ERP Digital License Management

Strategy to manage ERP Digital Licenses to avoid audit non-compliance

Authors

Gangesh Thakur & Jayaraman Kalaimani

ERP Digital License Management: Strategy to manage ERP Digital Licenses

Copyright © 2019 by Jayaraman Kalaimani

We dedicate this book to our colleagues and family

Table of Contents

Foreword

21st century is the mark of an I.T revolution with changes going on in the I.T Landscape. Especially with the advent of disruptive technologies such as AI, IoT, Robotic process automation, Block chain, SMAC technologies and on-demand enterprise etc. Today, Infrastructure as a Service (IaaS), Platform as a service (PaaS) or software-as-a-service (SaaS) is a reality. However, your I.T landscape has become autonomous with added complexities with several interfaces and the data flows from your core ERP system. With more automation and complexities to solve business problems, there are stringent requirements, policies, laws needed to manage software assets in the way we procure, consume, monitor and retire. Needless to state SAM governance plays a pivotal role in the organizations to avoid non-compliance.

Authors have done a brilliant job in consolidating various case studies without digressing from the core topic of software asset compliance and license management. This is very critical for organizations to leverage Industry best practices to strategize and avoid penalties imposed by editors due to non-compliance. As an executive, I reckon this is a valuable information for any I.T organization to manage software asset best practices.

I would like to congratulate the authors for the brilliant piece of work and it's useful for any executive to understand the importance of asset management practices with implementation guidelines.

Well done!

Subrata, Mandal

CIO, Aliaxis Group of Companies,

Bangalore,

India.

Foreword

The I.T Landscape has become more complex with several interfaces and the data flows from your core ERP system. In the world of multi-channel enabled for sourcing, supply chain, finance, marketing users have expanded access from mobile, smart platform. There is someone out there in the Organization who're responsible for managing assets, users and access, license compliance and audit. This is a very important topic in the digital era as organizations transforming into digital space will need dedicated teams to manage licenses. This book has arrived at the right time to help organizations to implement license best practices as they venture into transforming into Digital.

Well done authors to consolidate with real time case studies. I am sure 'ERP Digital License Management' book would help corporate executives to strategize license management in the priority list during their sprint cycle.

Arindam, Sen
Director at HCL Technologies,
Bangalore.
India.

Acknowledgements

We would like to thank Amazon for the opportunity to share the experiences with the world of Software asset consultants, software asset managers and corporate executives. It is a journey and digital license topic is still evolving with publisher tools to gauge current state of consumption with strict deadlines to achieve audit compliance.

A book of this size would not have been possible without the support of our colleagues, friends and family. Our sincere thanks to editorial team for the review and proofreading throughout the stages of this book.

We would like to thank all my colleagues for their enthusiasm and support for this project, and, finally to the Divine Space in us, thank you—for everything.

Introduction

The ERP Digital License Management is the hottest topic due to several companies transforming into Intelligent Enterprises. Every organization is riding the wave of transformation with new tools, methods implemented to automate key business processes. However, organizations are unable to manage asset life cycle and monitor licenses using metrics with a robust tool suite, thus end-up in outdated products in the landscape with the cost of maintenance and licenses shooting up every year. License management is neglected subject although constitute 50-70% of Total Cost of Operation. With the increasing trend of software-as-a-service (SAAS), license cost goes further in proportion. As businesses grew larger and complex in terms of key business processes, the underlying software systems became overly complex. The number of users from local increased to global with the advent of mobile channels.

Therefore, it is imperative for every organization to discuss software asset management which is planning, deployment, manage and retire along with periodic audit & compliance to mitigate the non-compliance risks and penalties. It is important to understand the contract from a neutral perspective. These risks may create enormous pressure during the audit reviews by the respective software editor. Any sign of non-compliance would lead to huge penalties and pull you from a strong negotiation position for additional license procurement. Hence, extreme care is required to industrialize the approach of metric based license usage policies to ensure absolute compliance, governance with risk mitigated planning and execution.

No wonder, software giants such as IBM, SAP, ORACLE, MICROSOFT, DASSAULT information technology companies servicing in multiple Industry verticals have geared up to the digital challenges. Most of the software companies have already evolved strategies for the Digital licensing model with a host of digital transformation companies providing tools, accelerators, and methods to implement best practices. With many more IOT device manufacturing companies offering devices with services integrating your manufacturing plants, thus turning into smart factories. These factories integrate seamlessly with your core ERP systems and access information real-time, perhaps software companies are driving innovation rapidly by enhancing their customer experience and these customers are in-turn equally excited to scale up in terms of operations, optimize resources. Thus, companies are investing in innovation strategy and creating value for their end-customers. For example. SAP S/4HANA, Microsoft Azure and Google services are all wonderful initiatives as they offer the entire platform as a service (PaaS) towards building up intelligent enterprises.

Just imagine a decade ago, a minor change to the existing I.T landscape would have taken a lot of resources in terms of efforts, time and financials. Hence, change management across various departments was very challenging. Today, it is done in a single click with updates activated to your core functions at the speed of light. Your business changes, I.T operations, innovations have become leaner in terms of cost, the speed of implementation with fewer resources. Thus, automation has paved the way for artificial intelligence, IoT devices, and security-enhanced to support your core business operations.

Large ERP companies have invested in Digital core technologies by way of acquisition of Digital technology companies and incentives to the engineers to promote a digital transformation journey within the enterprise. A recent acquisition of human capital management (HCM) on cloud platform service providers by SAP is an example of large ERP software companies acquiring smaller digital technology companies. This is one of the motivational factors for customers rapidly adopting digital enterprise best practices. Therefore, the product line is evolving into the digital enterprise on a cloud with seamlessly connected devices, ERP systems, and middleware that connects on-premises, cloud and device inputs to enable an integrated architecture to provide consumable services to the Industries. First time in the Industry, there is a major revolution happening with data transfers and the way information is consumed by the customers. These are phenomenal challenges in the I.T landscape to consolidate and understand the different licenses strategies evolved by these Editors to align and avoid any misconception. This would help organizations to remain nimble, understand the product line and licensing contracts. A lot of diligence is required in terms of maintaining an accurate inventory of products across different editors and licenses terms and conditions which is unique to the customers in the region.

The point is IT landscape is changing rapidly to move towards building your Intelligent enterprises by the way of evolutions. Hence, every organization is transforming into the next wave of Intelligent enterprise by using large enterprise solutions. These changes are inevitable, and none can resist. As part of the evolutions, it is imperative to focus on maximizing the value out of these software investments by the way of understanding the software rights usage, optimizing the usage and keep active monitoring of licenses by using tools, methods, and accelerators. This will be the only way to avoid penalties due to non-compliance, which may have legal consequences in your business. As an example, there were few lawsuits filed against many organizations using core ERP for B2C sales, which was not intended to be used in multiple channels. Today, as part of the Intelligent enterprises, it is inevitable to provide access to customers across multi-channels, devices, and access to your core ERP by understanding the software rights and your contracts with respective editors. This is one of the most important aspects of your legal, I.T teams validating your specific software contracts with software editors to avoid non-compliance. As a best practice, you'll need to have a dedicated software licenses compliance team managing overall compliance and audit requirements.

In one of the events in the year 2018 SAP TECHED Bangalore, the main theme was around SAP Intelligent Enterprise. SAP is constantly re-innovating itself to be the up-to-date trendsetter ahead of the competitors in the Industry. Whilst many software providers are setting up innovation labs, SAP is a pioneer in releasing ERP product suite for the new age digital technologies and processes. It's imperative to discuss digital licenses in a transparent manner to avoid huge penalties that may be imposed by the software providers. Hence, customer's need to be aware of the products procured and the sourcing team will need to read through the contractual terms and conditions. Luckily, SAP has started its' tools, services to keep it simple and transparent licenses though It's extremely complex, it is possible to set up a

11

license competency/compliance team to understand what you're paying for every year in terms of overall software licenses operational expenses (OpEx).

Most of the Industry experts were astonished by SAP's announcements on Digital access in the new age Digital Enterprise. Indeed, most of the Industries run their core applications using SAP software for more than 40 years. SAP has been helping companies run mission-critical business processes across all industries. SAP has transformed from an ERP software company to the Intelligent Enterprise platform for the future, and it has gained its market share by continuously re-engineering its products and solutions. Now, the challenges are aplenty for customers, partners those who run ERP software to keep up to the pace of licenses requirements of the digital evolution to ensure compliance in the evolving ERP Landscape. Hence, every company strives to set-up the compliance & audit team to manage software licenses and support audit requirements. In one of the case studies, SAP has claimed against a customer in October 2015, seeking huge penalties in license fees, in addition to fees charged as interest, for back-office support and maintenance, and an injunction.

The ERP Digital Licenses Management will help you to understand the asset management lifecycle and digital licenses model with emphasis on compliance and audit practices to avoid risks to the organization; however, it is not a replacement for regular audit or consulting. As a way forward, SAP is geared up for the transformation of legacy licensing model to the outcome-based software licensing. Each topic discussed in this book will explain the background information regarding the licensing strategies with specific case studies to help you drive changes within the organization as an SAP License leader. The following topics are covered with relevant case studies:

- Overview of software asset management (acquire, deploy, audit & compliance and retire)
- Common pitfalls of asset management, strategy to build a robust platform to manage licenses and mitigation
- License management methodology using tool, methods and process best practices
- License audit strategy to mitigate financial risks due to non-compliance
- Recommendations & Best practices

I.T compliance and risk management is a full-time dedicated effort to manage risks and compliance issues within the organization. The software asset management team is responsible for audit preparations and execution within the organization before the real audit conducted by the publisher. This is one of the main challenges faced by many organizations in preparing for the audit, looks like mayhem as they're simply not prepared. This would lead to inadvertent risks to your organization in terms of compliance issues and your ability to negotiate contracts with these software providers.

The main objectives of the ERP Digital Licenses Management book are to discuss various challenges in digital licenses management with software-as-a-Services (SaaS) or on-premises (On-premises) perpetual licensing model, especially in digital enterprises. Every organization is striving to transform into the digital economy, therefore it is important to set up digital software asset management practices with key performance indicators (KPI) to procure, monitor and negotiate the best value for money. It's a complex landscape, however with a proper due-diligence and understanding various digital product suites with careful planning and monitor, it is possible to implement the best practices in software licenses.

License Agreements Pitfalls

Most of the organization pay huge license fees to software database vendors. Here is an example of license cost split by database system deployment for hardware, software and storage. Some of the Key takeaways based on the following survey is to identify license cost of the database is substantial up to 80% goes to software application vendor. So, the question is what are the early warning signs that you would look out for.

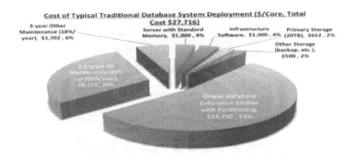

13

Let us explore common pitfalls in the software license management. Perhaps, you can group it to components that attribute as core factors of compliance such as rules, regulations, laws and regulatory stated in the compliance critical factors.

This book is directed at Corporate Executives, IT Program Managers, Project Managers, Compliance & Audit teams, Software Asset Management (SAM) team, Operations, Sourcing, Finance, Infrastructure leads, Administrators, Transition Managers, and Business Leaders to understand the risks involved in terms of audit compliance and mitigate by transforming to the Digital Licensing Era. This book would also help the CFO/IT/IS department to make the right ERP software licensing decisions with deeper knowledge and understanding of the licensing compliance requirements with case studies of common pitfalls. End of the chapters, you will gain insights on the following points:

a. Gain understanding of asset management lifecycle & license methodology
b. Managing an effective license position based on your contract with publishers and the negotiation strategy
c. Avoiding risks due to non-compliance and penalties
d. Help you gain a deeper understanding of license compliance requirements
e. Eliminating license audit non-compliance risks with Industry best practices
f. Mitigating risks and effective negotiation strategy with editors
g. Adopting organization-wide licenses policies
h. Implications of digital transformation with respect to licenses
i. Focusing on the Omnichannel users connecting to the core ERP with evolving license policies
j. Agile in adopting various measurements with internal audit capabilities with metrics

Diligent planning would help the organizations to benefit from the outcome-based licensing model to negotiate with ERP editors (SAP) to get the best offer. Digital licensing is not just the technology change; it is the future vision of SAP ECC into S/4HANA to benefit vast customer pool, who are using technology as the backbone. Hence, it is therefore important for both licensors and licensees to incorporate proper controls in place to check the use of an organization's software assets. This should be done to not only avoid financial setbacks but also reduce risks for infringing entities.

■   ■   ■

Chapter 1: Introduction to Digital Licenses

The main objectives of this chapter are to give you an overview of the software asset lifecycle and digital License compliance with the current challenges faced by Organizations to keep track of software asset inventory and audit requirements for compliance. We would discuss on a survey conducted by BSA along with Gartner insights on asset management practices.

One of our clients embarked on the most ambitious project to prepare the organization for the ERP Licenses audit, which was a daunting task by the end of the financial year. You may imagine the complexities involved in consolidating data across various departments in your organization to present a single view of the compliance & audit team. The situation might get trickier with the external auditors as you may end-up scrambling for data points to just your non-compliance. It is like an attorney trying to prove his case with evidence. As you know software license is a legal agreement for use of the software with specific terms and conditions.

When proprietary software is bought, only the license is restricted to access as mentioned in the software user rights contract. The proprietary rights, however, remain with the software publisher. It is important to plan operational governance to evaluate usage on a regular basis. With digital products and solutions emerging every day, it is important that the industry is aware of licensing pitfalls to avoid any infringement of their intellectual property. For a licensee organization, it is important to understand the contract and license utilization to be managed more diligently.

You'll need to understand that license is a major revenue stream for the publisher, which is an opportunity for upselling. As a result, publishers are driving software compliance audits for their customers more rigorously than ever. Typically, an organization faces an average of three compliance audits per year. For example. SAP does it annually, however, it has necessary rights to an audit anytime. Typically, compliance audit will take two to three months to complete and requires significant time and effort on the part of companies. Compliance audits would generally lead to the identification of non-compliance, which may lead to penalties. Therefore, over-consumption of licenses and inventory analysis is required as per the contracts with software publisher. Any such non-compliance of software may lead to legal consequences. Therefore, it is therefore important for both licensors and licensees to incorporate KPI's to monitor and control on a periodic basis.

The key goals of the license compliance and audit program are the following:

- Identify non-compliance risks and baseline usage to monitor non-compliance
- Establish best practices as per ERP standard auditory requirements as a mitigation plan. For example. SAP licenses?
- How much money $$ can we possibly save in the future by contract extensions or reclassifications to digital core licenses.

- How fast can we prepare the organization for the ERP audit, which can be autonomous?
- How do we prepare for the ERP licenses audit requirements and negotiation position such as SAP?
- What are the key non-compliance risks and mitigation plan?
- Clarify digital licenses and publisher's road map of licenses for direct and indirect access to the core software that is licensed
- If you identify non-compliance, then consult the best possible ways to optimize

Each of your employees is responsible from a compliance point of view in consuming licenses appropriately. Your software policy document must highlight the best practices. It's important to understand each of the above questions in detail to mitigate non-compliance risks, prepare your organization for compliance & audit practices, and maximize contract negotiation opportunities with respective editors. As an asset manager or ERP License manager or an Executive, you have a daunting task of pulling all the strings together to summarize your organization current licenses compliance position to state to the executive speech on your compliance level with remediation approach in a nutshell. Hence, it is necessary to deliver a license dashboard with a summary view of all products in the landscape with metrics.

Often, I.T Program Managers find it difficult to assess license compliance position due to lack of accurate inventory of licenses. If you do not know what products that you're paying for due to several applications in the Landscape, then, in the end, managing the entitlements with editors will become challenging and risky too. Eventually, you'd end up paying more license fee plus penalties based on audit results to the respective provider.

Hence, it is prudent to start planning early, set up the best practices and governance to manage the ERP licenses compliance & audit practices to mitigate risks due to non-compliance. As a best practice, we advocate consolidating usage analysis and review the past year history to determine the current stock situation, with analysis of forecasts based on the projects pipeline. This step would guarantee you to monitor usage and to assess the scope of additional requirements. In a broader perspective, a license management program is essential to identify current inventory, forecast additional license requirements based on the new projects in the pipeline with proper governance to ensure compliance.

This asset management and license monitor initiative would help your organization to remain compliant and the respective teams will be more organized with proper governance. This would avoid a mad rush at the last hour during the audit with editors. Often, technical teams use licenses without even realizing the impact due to non-compliance and the software user rights agreement. This is due to a lack of communication between departments. Perhaps, your sourcing team is not aware of consumption on a quarterly basis, leading to forecasts that are not accurate. Hence, sourcing and delivery teams in your organization must align and organize quarterly reviews with software asset management (SAM) team dashboard for licenses to ensure compliance across various software in the landscape. Therefore, an internal audit to monitor license position is essential to avoid penalties.

Perhaps, you're unable to derive the value out of the I.T investments, which may lead to overspending on I.T software products, thus impacting your revenues as you may not be aware of the asset life cycle. Hence, it becomes complex task to consolidate assets with current licenses position without an entire overhaul of studying each of these interface applications connected to your core ERP in the digital landscape. Let us explore software asset management insights provided by Gartner.

IT Asset Life Cycle

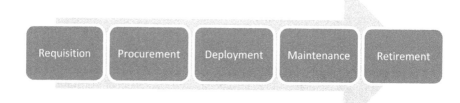

Source: Gartner

IT Asset Management (ITAM) is a framework and set of process to manage license and contract aspects of assets through their life cycle. The key elements to realize the value of IT assets management are:

a.   Focus on financial, contractual and physical data
b.   The asset life cycle and
c.   A process framework

The objectives of IT asset management are to ensure the assets are managed effectively from beginning to the end to achieve highest return on investment. Your landscape may include complex hardware, software, network to support business critical operations. Hence, your assets will need constant upgrade to keep up-to-date and current. The key functions of ITAM includes:

- Financial (purchase, cost and supplier contracts)
- Contractual (terms & conditions, entitlement) &
- Physical (ownership, assignment, location etc)

Garnter identifies five stages of asset management as stated above. The actual cycle of an asset starts from the reguisition phase as higlighted. Gartner estimated aroudn 35% of organizations achieved desired maturity levels in ITAM process. The ITAM maturity levels increases with the process automation using tools and automation with ability to manage financial, contractual and physical data, integration with adjacent IT management tools and business systems. For example, Microsoft Provance solution provides an integrate ITAM solution for managing assets effectively. There is always a debate on the % cloud adoption, which means what applications can be migrated to cloud or remain as on-premises. Let us look at the following analysis report to compare SaaS vs. On-Premises applications with cost implications. However, the decision to migrate to cloud depends on organization policies.

License costs Bespoke (On-Premise) vs. SaaS

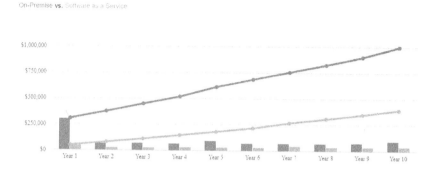

The above graph higlights the difference in terms of license expenses year-on-year. Typically, package software implementation is expense with customization expenses and upfront network setup, hardware and database costs.

Hypothetical data points for the above graph:

Description	On-Premises	Cloud (SaaS)
ERP Software Upfront Investment (CapeX)	$ 250, 000	0
Maintenance costs per Annum (OpeX)	$ 50, 000	$ 15,000
Contract Validity	3 years	2 years
Customization	$ 15000	0
Hardware Expenses	$ 25, 000	0
Installation & Setup	$ 5000	$ 1000

Typically for on-premises perpetual licenses, there is an upfront investments for hardware, software installation expenses. If you're installating an ERP system, there is a huge upfront investments for securing your own hardware, software and database licenses which is assumed here as $ 250, 000 USD upfront capital expenses (capex) with 25% operational expenses. Now, this is where there is a significant savings from an SaaS model, where you do not have to make an upfront

20

investments. Instead, you'd end-up paying for what you'd eventually use. In this case, let's call out a subscription fee of $ 25,000/annum with an increment by 15% after 3 years price increase term. This would yield significant benefits as highlighted in the graph above. There is a significant return on investments (ROI) derived by the subscription based software consumption model. Lets take a closer look at the insights from Gartner based on the increased software expenses with bespoke code adding to the maintenance costs. Let's explore BSA Global software survey to analyze % compliance in software licenses.

Gartner predicted that overall spending on software is expected to increase to US$326 billion in 2016 from US $ 310 billion in 2015 Gartner insights

BSA Global Software Survey

Today, the World is shifting to the digital economy at a rapid pace. Therefore, most enterprises run transactional processing using interfaces that may connect to core ERP as business to business (B2B) and business to customer (B2C) with integrated analytics processing capabilities. In either of these scenarios, partners, customers and suppliers may connect seamlessly to core applications using IoT or mobile devices leading to a synchronous or asynchronous mode of communication. In an Intelligent enterprise, there are various actors in the ecosystem seamlessly accessing data in your core ERP either directly or indirectly using multiple channels of data access from core ERP.

As stated below in the BSA Global software survey conducted in 2016, 39% of software was not properly licensed. Going forward, this trend will increase due to a lack of a robust governance process for monitoring licenses. This may end up in over-consumption or unutilized licenses, lack of retirement plan etc.

With the increasing number of devices connected to ERP, customers, partners, and suppliers access your core ERP using smart devices and the bandwagon of IIOT devices accessing information from ERP is increasing day-by-day. With devices talking to various interconnected IoT's, sensors passing data across devices and bots interacting with customers, there are a plethora of activities happening in your landscape. Several B2B customers access orders information from a portal or a mobile interface are not even measured as an outcome activity performed by the user. Hence, there is a huge GAP between the number of licenses procured vs. several licenses consumed from a compliance point of view.

21

The irony is that most of these software editors would allow users access until the audit, perhaps this is a strategy for more sales. In case of non-compliance identified by the software vendor, it may lead to huge penalties imposed to the customers, which would lead to several penalties for additional usage. As a customer, you may end up paying the penalties, and lose the privileges of negotiated price. Hence it is imperative to check your current licenses stock in terms of Direct, Indirect usage to the core ERP to remain compliant.

The main objectives of ERP's digital license method are to support customers in maintaining digital license compliance and meet audit requirements without much difficulty in a transparent way. Indeed, as a matter of fact, most of the customers DO NOT keep track of these indirect users or even direct access in the ever-growing digital landscape with so many users connected from various devices. With the advent of Machine Learning (ML), Artificial Intelligence (AI) the current position for the license manager's managing software licenses could be even more challenging due to the increased number of the disparate systems that read and/or write as an asynchronous or bi-synchronous mode of communications. In the recent study, a lot of bots intend to support customer services is triggering information extraction from the core ERP systems, however, there was no accountability of these bot usage. This could perhaps get a little overwhelming to measure the users count. If you're worried about the **'INDIRECT'** users, those who are accessing ERP from various interfaces in your landscape, it is time to consolidate a repository of information. Let's look at the license compliance trend published during 2009-14 by Gartner as illustrated below.

License Compliance Trend analysis

Courtesy: Gartner survey

As illustrated in the above Gartner survey, SAP has been instrumental in minimizing risks due to non-compliance by providing necessary tools to support audit requirements for customers. However, the recent survey results from Gartner indicates a growing trend of non-compliance with SAP customers to 18-20%. This may indicate usage due to increased complexity in the landscape or perhaps due to lack of understanding the software user rights. These risks must be categorized as direct, indirect and further analyzed to mitigate compliance challenges. Hence, SAP is supplementing with tools such as USMM for direct license assessment, LMBI for business objects & ENGINE for indirect measurement with metrics. Customers are finding new ways to extend the use of their digital core by giving access to business partners and consumers via third-party applications, and they are increasingly connecting to automated systems, IoT devices, and bots.

It is exciting to witness all these digital age advances and how customers are using enterprise software to transform their businesses. However, pricing models for enterprise software designed in the 20th Century have remained relatively the same across the industry and are not optimal for this new type of digital access, which the industry has coined "indirect access".

SAP's ERP pricing model was designed for using the system directly. For example, we have 100 users who work in ERP day-in and day-out by logging into the system directly. This is a simple use case. Therefore, SAP charged licenses per named user accessing data in the system. However, there may be professional, light professional, employee, technical usage of the system based on the profile of the user. For example. A plant user may be confined to the product order status only,

23

whereas an ADMIN user may functionally or technically be responsible across domains. Similarly, a purchase order department user is only interested in creating, updating purchase orders (PO's) and he may perform only a limited set of transactions in SAP.

Therefore, SAP has priced usage of **NAMED** users based on the profile categorized into Professional, Light professional, Technical, Business and Employer etc. by analyzing the profile and actual transaction usage. You'll receive detail information in the SAP contract with extensive notes on the software user rights. This is very important document that describes the software user rights with profiles. This user-based pricing works well for direct human access because it is predictable and well understood. However, it is not easy to apply when the ERP system is used indirectly (e.g., by a user logging into another application that then uses the power of SAP Digital Core to execute the business process) or digitally (e.g., when a device or a bot uses the system, and not a human user). This has led to an ambiguous interpretation of use and too unproductive discussions over what counts as users. The ambiguity has also led to inconsistent sales and audit practices that have ultimately shaken some of our customers' trust.

With a wide array of purchasing options such as perpetual licensing, unlimited licensing, subscription-based licensing, true-up and burn-down options, it could become difficult for companies to decide on which option they should go for. Lack of Internal controls, tracking of compliance and prohibiting the use of unauthorized software usage may lead to significant financial exposure. Further, tracking software license compliance cannot be a manual exercise, as the IT environment for most companies is dynamic and changes drastically in a matter of days. Automation and use of technology are the most important aspects of enabling proper governance and control.

The new licensing models apart from the traditional perpetual licensing models (which used to generally be on a per user, per CPU, per instance or per virtual machine basis), technological advances have brought in new services, which are broadly termed as "cloud" or "cloud computing." Cloud computing includes various services, such as Software as a Service (SaaS), Infrastructure as a Service (IaaS) and Platform as a Service (PaaS). The payment in these services is generally on a "pay-as-you-use" basis and is also called as "subscription licensing." Globally, there has been a rapid adoption of cloud computing and cloud-based infrastructure in the past couple of years. Many publishers now offer their traditional software products in a cloud-based environment covering both hardware and software for a subscription fee.

However, organizations need to be careful while moving applications to a cloud setup. Applications that have a sizeable amount of interplay between the organization and the external world, software that has periodic peaks of use and software that is dependent on internet access are ideal to be moved on to a SaaS model. On the other hand, applications where speedy processing of data is required or where legal contractual terms limit hosting of data externally may not be suitable for a SaaS model. Further, as many global companies increasingly develop cloud-based offerings, they need to develop and design robust cloud-based licenses, including on-demand licensing models. Low understanding in the developer community on a scope and open source obligations: Developers use various software for development purposes.

Generally, developers have permission to access and download various software, especially open source. When developing software, open source software may be used. Not all open source software is free of charge. Developers need to be cognizant of the nuances of open source license terms and conditions.

Many software programs are available on the internet as trial versions. If use is continued after the trial period, the software becomes chargeable. Organizations should, therefore, have proper controls and frameworks in place to manage the software programs that are being used for development to avoid infringement of copyrights. Sometimes, trial or test versions of developer tools cannot be used to develop commercial offerings. For instance, a company developing software using a trial or test version should check that the underlying software is properly licensed and has the correct commercial terms before offering the product for sale. It should also consider indemnity coverage for any third-party claim on the developer tools. Now let us explore the importance of a robust Software asset management License dashboard as illustrated below.

SAM (software asset management) License Dashboard

A typical license dashboard as illustrated below will demonstrate the following:

License Dashboard

License Dashboard will help in consolidating your current license position such as all software asset tracking with detailed usage and billing. It inlcudes alert services for any service overage. A hugely important feature License Dashboard Portal that offer full visibility of your compliance and usage for the entire fleet within a single centralized view; by consolidating data from multiple sources in one place.

Some of the key features of licenses dashboard include the following:

1. Monitor assets with license dashboard portal
2. Report platform consumption
3. Manipulate data and save customized reports
4. Monthly trends / consumption analysis
5. See complex Cloud usage in a single unified view

Case study

Our client used a combination of on-premises, SaaS and cloud based architecture with lot of bespoke code. This is the main challenge as license cost increases depending on the perpetual licenses. If you have a lot of custom applications, then rest assured, your maintenance would go very high for maintaing and upgrading your code in-line with the version upgrade done by editors. This is a critical task for SAP customers, where changes to the standard code, program exits, custom code will need hefty maintenance costs. Hence, most of the customers are switching to standard code in cloud based consumption model with SAP or revamp their business practices to align to the best practices.

This is the common practice in most of the scenario, whenever a customer upgrades the SAP software, they try to migrate the custom code to the standard code to leverage the benefits of standardization in terms of maintenance costs. On the contrary, if you application is a standalone, then you would end-up design, develop and implementing in-house without an external license cost, except for the hardware, network and database expenses. However, your maintenance costs would shoot up in the longer run. In our view, it is better to go with standardized and proven solution with Industry best practices without much time to implement. Indeed, you should select software that is already proven in the Industry with best practices implementation. A package software solution is the best way to adopt Industry best practices, however with an additional premium for your high performance softare engine. Gone are the days of developing your own software for a specific requirement, unless your totally niche in the Industry with no standard software available for your unique requirements.

In the manufacturing company that we are talking about, For example, core applications run using SAP and Engineering applications were hosted internally by the client, whilst the HCM systems such as SAP Success Factor and SAP Concur for expense management, a third party payroll application hosted on-cloud were managed as subscription based on cloud. This is one of the hybrid approahces, where you would leverage SaaS applications and core Engineering and Manufacturing operations software as on-premises solution. Perhaps, this may sound as a conservative approach. However, if you look at the benchmark analysis report from Gartner, most of the companies are embrasing digital technologies on-cloud, which is much cheaper than the on-premises solution. In terms of license benefits, you must do a cost-benefits analysis as perpetual SAP S/4HANA licenses might be expensive due to additional HANA appliance requirements, which is an upfront requirement. However S/4HANA might be log cheaper in terms of upfront investments, but customers will need to carefully assess their roadmap in order to arrive at the best possible solution, as S/4HANA on cloud might be expensive in the long-run. Today, market provides a lot of option to utilize platform-as-a-service using SAP HANA Cloud Platform (HCP) Amazon web services (AWS), Google Cloud platform (GCP), Oracle Cloud Platform (OCP) or Microsoft Azure platform which are excellent and futuristic hosting platforms to launch your organization to the Digital platform. It may be prudent to launch a detailed due-diligence phase with cost-benefits analysis to finalize the best possible solution that fits your organizations goals and long-term roadmap.

Based on your organizations goals, you can plan to utilize cloud based options. Most of the clients are concerned about the security protocols and GDPR compliance, which are taken care by the service providers. A lot of clients have migrated critical applications to Microsoft AZURE or Amazon AWS or Google. The future of I.T would be manated entirely on-Cloud to avoid the capital expenses, however the challenges are regarding restructuring internal I.T organization and policies to manage service providers effectively.

Summary

In this chapter, you've studied the overview of asset management, license compliance and audit requirements with the emphasis on best practices such as robust dashboard to consolidate asset data from various sources with insights from Gartner and a case study. This would help you manage the compliance and audit requirements. Now, let's look at the holistic approach by assessing common pitfalls of digital license management with case studies in the next chapter.

■ ■ ■

Chapter 2: Common License Pitfalls

The main objectives of this chapter are to discuss common license pitfalls with risks and mitigation. With these risks escalating every day, corporates are focusing on best practices to mitigate compliance risks. It's everyone's responsibilities to ensure successful license audit and compliance to avoid any legal consequences. As a matter of fact, SAP had penalized a major brewery company in Europe for breach of license agreements. Hence it is extremely important for large organizations to build a practice to manage software assets, comprising of SAM managers and legal experts to review every statement carefully to avoid any major risks to the business.

It is challenging if the I.T landscape has a multi-tenant infrastructure, as it is difficult to manage software licenses which may remain as a blind spot. Since the shift in the fundamental infrastructure has changed from on-premises to cloud-hosted services there are lots of licenses parameters that you'll need to take care of. For example. You may have partially TEST and DEVELOPMENT system that may still exist in your landscape as on-premise infrastructure, whereas productive environment may land-up as cloud infra. Hence, these strategic decisions would change your license buying options based on the return on investments (ROI) derived from this expenditure. You must carefully evaluate every single option prior to arriving at the final and best solution.

The enterprises using software may be exposed to risks and penalties due to lack of visibility in the ongoing maintenance charges such as over-consumption of licenses they obtain for the internal users and customers, suppliers. The real issue is the lack of transparency in terms of accessing SAP applications, with the flow of data from the systems via customer portals to the individual customers in the digital economy. Even worse, most of the executives are not aware of the requirements of the digital license as the application landscape is accessed by the business to consumers (B2C) via portal interfaces. This is where the concept of indirect access introduced by ERP software vendors to cover any consumer accessing details on a website or placing an order or tracking delivery if any of the information has been generated by, or delivered through, any SAP software, however indirectly.

Although SAP at present appears to be only pursuing Business-to-Business (B2B) usage – for example, by distributors and sales representatives – SAP's wide license terms can extend to Business-to-Consumers (B2C) customers. In the global economy, internal users, external customers, partners and suppliers access the application using mobile, tablets, laptops over the internet seamlessly to access and update information as necessary. For example, creating a sales order using mobile is a good example how it is simple for the users to place an order in the ERP system, however tracking such licenses is complex due to the nature of the entitlements managed with the respective software provider. These contracts vary between customers and there is no one-size licenses contract that would fit everyone. Indeed, SAP's contracts are much more complex in this context. Hence, most of the clients request for a professional firm to investigate entitlements and ensure auditory compliance is managed at regular intervals.

More and more people are collaborating effectively using digital media and the world is now truly transforming into one global digital village. With the advent of technologies, faster core processors, enterprise-scale smartphones emerging into the digital world, there is a lot more people can do than ever in human history. As Darwin's theory of fittest of survival goes, the enterprise would survive by leveraging technologies to migrate rapidly into the digital world. The digital license program is an initiative from SAP to mitigate compliance risks and support audit best practices. Today, CRM software is gaining proximity to social media with tightly integrated into the core ERP enterprise landscape.

Well, one of the common pitfalls in license management is lack of analyzing benefits of migrating to cloud infrastructure, leading to increased license costs. For example, if your applications are partially running in the cloud, you may still need middleware and security protocols to ensure data exchange between your applications on-cloud to on-premise software applications. Therefore, we advocate a proof-of-concept study to analyze cost-benefits, without risking the overall business objectives. Keeping data security constraints in mind and your organizational policies, you may embark on a digital journey with a 5-year roadmap and start in a sequential manner, rather than the big bang to keep the business risks to the minimal. If you're a new organization, you'd perhaps want to start in the cloud, which is a blessing in disguise. No questions asked in terms of deriving cost-benefits, however existing enterprises with a laundry list of applications, interfaces, and data exchanges, perhaps will need to avoid **BIG BANG** implementation approach. There is a lot of potential in moving to the cloud.

In terms of software and hardware licenses, the cloud may prove to be cheaper depending on the choices selected such as Amazon Web Services (AWS), Microsoft Azure or S/4HANA on Cloud (HCP) or SAP hosted on AWS. It depends on your organizational goals and strategy; careful planning is required to assess real cost-benefits derived based on detailed analysis and case study references in a similar industry. Now let us explore the common pitfalls with examples.

This was the case when SAP filed a lawsuit in one of the customer situations due to non-compliance. The customer is one of the largest brewery company based in Europe with global operations. The core ERP was SAP with several interfaces. Some of these B2C portal users were able to create sales orders directly from the portal interface with a transaction triggered by the user via remote functional calls (RFC) to connect directly to SAP and create new orders. There were over 10,000+ users with thousands or orders created every month.

Apparently, the above-identified situation resulted in several non-SAP users raising orders from the portal. Almost several thousands of orders were raised every month. Hence, in the claim, SAP AG had stated that the customer has used the software inappropriately and caused damages by accessing SAP data from a third-party portal without a proper SAP licensed user accessing information in the system. Hence, there was a huge revenue loss incurred by SAP and they backdated usage of the customer B2C portal users and arrived at close to $ 10M (Ten Million) UKI pounds as a penalty. Indeed, this was an alarming case study to realize the impact of the unethical practices conducted by the customer. I hope this situation does not occur in any of your customer cases.

The only way to mitigate risk is by setting robust audit practices backed up by software to monitor, control and optimize your usage. We have identified major pitfalls in managing digital licenses as highlighted below in terms of people, process & technology by impacting the key factors of compliance listed below:

Critical Success Factors

As illustrated above, Compliance encompasses the following eight core components with pitfalls identified in each of the core compliance areas as highlighted in the below table:

SNO	Compliance factor	Pitfalls
1	Requirements	Lack of scope
2	Rules	Lack of understanding liability terms and conditions
3	Standards	Lack of established metrics & testing
4	Governance	Lack of process, governance

5	Regulations	Lack of renewal terms
6	Transparency	Lack of communication
7	Policy	Lack of established policies
8	Law	Lack of statement of work & Lack of legal team internally review

As you realize, non-compliance will lead to several financial, contractual, legal & audit risks. Let us explore common license pitfalls leading to non-compliance

In this section, we will explore critical success factors with pitfalls in each of these critical areas as detailed below:

1. Requirements

a. Lack of Scope definition

It's important to understand the scope of the license is very important by I.T and the business teams to avoid conflicts with the supplier. Often sourcing team is responsible for negotiating the contract without realizing the software user rights. Hence, you'll need to review the software user rights with the technical teams to analyze the contract in detail such as employee profile with mapping in terms of software user rights. In one of the instances, we observed extensive usage of SAP professional usage for a procurement user. This is a huge waste of money as it costs more than the procurement user.

Perhaps, a procurement manager will need a Light SAP professional license access, however, even if he is entitled to do more, he would never use the software extensively. Hence, your security policies should be an integral part of user creation and assignments. A standard contract may look good for sourcing, which may not be the case for I.T teams. The licensee must closely consider the scope of the desired license. Whether it will be an enterprise-wide license, per seat license, or concurrent user license, the licensee must confirm the licensing entity and scope of use.

For example, in one of the classic examples, supplier team, who're affiliates of a client company agreed to use the software under the same license or allow the

33

parent entity to use a license entered by a subsidiary. This is a clear breach of the license agreement. This is exactly where SAP has advised clients to use '**ENGINE**' license agreement for **INDIRECT** access.

This would allow users to continue to use SAP without a '**NAMED**' direct access in the relevant environments. In addition, it should be clear that the licensee's authorized third-party contractors and perhaps even outsourcers will also have the right to use the software without running afoul of the licensing terms. Point is to bring in transparency to the usage from a licensee point-of-view to ensure both direct and indirect usage is monitored.

SAP provides ENGINE licenses to mitigate the risks of non-compliance due to Indirect licenses. For example. If you're creating many sales orders triggered by an external portal application, then each of these indirect users will need either NAMED indirect access or ENGINE that quantifies a specific pool of documents that can be created. In this case, let's say SALES ORDER engine type procured by the client would help them process 10-20k sales orders per year. Similarly, you've different types of ENGINE licenses such as PROCURE-TO-PAY (P2P), ORDER-TO-CASH (O2C) etc.

For SAP middleware products such as SAP NetWeaver PI, the measurement is based on CPU utilization. For example, user rights are measured by the no. of CPU's deployed.

2. Standards
a. Lack of Acceptance Testing Rights

It's a common practice to split the payments to the licensor based on the acceptance criteria. Any software implementation of any level of difficulty should include clear acceptance testing rights for the licensee. In SAP implementations, testing would encompass security testing phase prior to sign-off. In this phase, the team will thoroughly test all scenarios with appropriate roles to ensure alignment. Our recommendation is to align roles assignments with licenses to be included as part of the test phase to avoid non-compliance due to extended use of higher license category.

Ideally, the licensee should not be obligated to pay any license or support fees until acceptance testing has been performed and the software has passed the tests.

Vendors will often point to the software warranty as the licensee's best tool to ensure properly functioning software, but that relies on the licensee then making a claim under the agreement for breach of warranty and may require formal legal action before a resolution is to reach. A robust software testing practices must ensure all rights appropriately test and functioning prior to acceptance sign-off by evaluating all criteria is met.

3. Rules

You must gain complete understanding of the financials, terms and conditions mentioned in the contract. A lot of content in the software user rights will need to be reviewed in detail to understand the entitlement. You must know what you're paying for and the options to interchange with a different category of licenses based on the usage pattern. Also, your current financials including CapEx and OpEx paid need to be tracked to ensure additional procurement can entitle for a similar discount.

4. Regulations

a. Lack of Renewal Terms

Software licenses often have initial terms of one to three years and it's imperative that the licensee contemplate and define pricing terms for any potential renewal terms. Typically, SAP licenses will charge based on the category of licenses with capex and year-on-year operational expenses (OpEx) charged as % of the capital expenditure (CapEx) user licenses cost per user. For example. For example. SAP Professional user might be on the top of the category with more rights and its expensive. On the lower side, there might be employee user rights that are cheaper. However, the licensee has spent significant money and time choosing a software package, implementing the software, and training its employees and then the software vendor. Hence, it is the responsibility of the licensee to ensure appropriate use of software rights based on the agreement.

5. Policies

a. Lack of realizing the limitation of Liability

These are legal terms and condition, which most of the companies overlook. It is very important to understand the liability clause such as indemnification obligation, exclude indirect damages from their potential liability,

35

and cap their liability for direct damages. But the fact is that the party best suited to control and limit potential damages related to possible infringement of any third party's intellectual property rights by the software is the software vendor.

Therefore, there should be a clear obligation for indemnifying the licensee in the event of claim regarding such possible infringement by the software or the licensee's use of the software and that indemnification obligation should be carved out from any limitation of liability. There may be few terms that are agreeable based on the use of the software as described in the documentation and other exceptions to the indemnification obligation, but in the end, the indemnification should be clear and comprehensive.

b.   Lack of support Term / New Products

You must ensure the exit criteria is well defined, in case you want to migrate to different software. Hence as a client, you have the right to migrate as per terms and contracts or request for any replacement software during the support term; although that may be a less than ideal solution depending on what that transition to the new software entails.

6.   Governance

a.   Lack of collaborative approach

Let's explore various challenges due to the lack of collaboration between teams leading to licenses non-compliance.
- Lack of dedicated leadership focus. Not prioritizing license topics in executive meetings may lead to overlooking many software asset license issues.
- Lack of dedicated licenses practices team with defined RACI with stakeholders from Projects, Operations, Software Asset Management (SAM) and Admins to support respective tasks
- Lack of consultations with internal legal, sourcing teams to ensure compliance. Often it is important to understand from a neutral point-of-view with a legal consultant validating the proposal.
- Lack of data governance, policy implementation by the internal I.T audit teams may lead to a lack of ownership of user assignments and thus leading to non-compliance
- Lack of ownership due to undefined roles & responsibilities across departments (RACI). Often, sourcing may work

individually without validating contracts from a technical point-of-view leading to non-compliance

- Matrix organization with several teams working without proper ownership of respective systems

b. Lack of process driven approach

Lack of process may lead to several non-compliance issues as stated below:

- Lack of license metrics leading to non-compliance. For example, if you don't know how to measure license utilization, then it is even worse as you don't have the inventory with measurement criteria agreed with the vendor
- Lack of quality check on licenses availability forecasts to ensure compliance. Often, we noticed a lack of controls such as internal audit practices and usage policies enforced to avert non-compliance
- Lack of internal audit controls, the procedure to prepare teams for the final audit
- Lack of risk assessment and control methods, thus leading to issues including financial losses. Mostly non-compliance issues are noticed by the end of the year when the audit is already in progress
- Lack of control procedures for new users, user activation and de-activation policies implementation.

d. Lack of automation

Let's explore risks due to lack of automatized approach.

- Lack of automated licenses inventory of the software products & suites using a tool-based approach to measure usage with defined metrics
- Lack of managing data-driven entitlements up-to-date may lead to misunderstandings with the vendor
- Lack of traceability of the software purchases against the Purchase Request, Purchase Order. Most customers do not even realize the purchase or material code to refer to the source of the master agreement and subsequent changes. This will result in a lot of stress during the audit
- Lack of visibility to the amendments to contracts such as exchange offerings on specific product suites. Mostly exchange terms are discussed during the negotiation phase and contract

signed with high-level details. This will lead to a lack of clarity in subsequent terms and conditions.

- Lack of regular contact with the respective vendor account manager to assess the current licenses position
- Lack of disclosure to avoid penalties may lead to legal issues and unethical behaviour
- Lack of regular internal audit with well-defined workflows
- Lack of KPI's to measure processes with metrics

7. Transparency

a. Lack of clarity regarding Maintenance and Support

As stated before, the software vendor will often point to the software warranty and perhaps support obligations when the licensee looks for a remedy related to the failure of the software to meet the requirements of the agreement. In addition to the acceptance testing rights, it's also important to confirm that the warranty and support terms are appropriate. Often, we find software user rights documents are difficult to interpret.

For example, any language stating that the vendor needs to only attempt to remedy any non-conformance should be scrutinized closely. If that warranty states that the vendor will use "best efforts" to address software bugs, then the licensee may end up with software that has unresolved issues for a very long period with the only remedy to argue that the vendor isn't using enough effort to resolve the issue. It's preferable to have language stating that the failure to resolve an issue that affects the licensee's use of the software will trigger certain licensee rights, including termination for cause if the issue is not resolved in an agreed period.

8. LAW

a. Lack of clarity regarding Termination Rights

You must ensure clarity in terms of the existing clause. The licensee should contemplate the termination or expiration of the agreement and verify that the agreement reflects the licensee's conditions in either event. Depending on the type of software at issue, there may be a desire to have a data extract from the software prior to shut down, the licensee may wish to engage the vendor in assisting with the transition to replacement software, or the licensee may wish to confirm that the vendor will destroy all copies of the licensee's data in its possession soon after termination or expiration.

b. Lack of Detailed Statement of Work

A statement of work that is part of the license agreement is frequently overlooked by the licensee's legal team. But it's imperative that the SOW is reviewed carefully both to confirm that there is no legal language that conflicts with the terms of the body of the agreement and to ensure that the business terms in the document are sufficiently detailed and measurable to clearly set forth the obligations of both parties. A vague statement of work or one that relies on the parties to work out the details following execution is of little value and does nothing to aid in the timely installation of the software.

c. Lack of common Agreements

Most software vendors rely on separate agreements for the license terms, installation services, and ongoing support services resulting in multiple separate agreements defining the relationship. Hence, you must define a clear relationship between each of these agreements and confirm that you've clear rights to terminate related agreements in the event one is terminated for cause or otherwise. Therefore, the licensee should also consider carefully any limitations of liability or other limitations tied to the value of one agreement on its own.

License Risks and Mitigation

Listed below are some of the key outstanding risks are highlighted:

Risk	Category	Impact	Description
Commercial	Finance	High	Penalties paid to publishers due to non-compliance
Legal Non-compliance	Legal	Very High	Sanctions may be imposed due to non-compliance over an extended period
Critical business process	Business	High	Lack of alternation solution for key business process
Software Asset Management	Business	Medium	Lack of internal controls leading to non-compliance
Data & Security	Business	High	Lack of internal data security policy & data theft prevention

As highlighted, it is important to mitigate each of the risks highlighted above. First is the legal to avoid non-compliance risks and then the optimization or internal controls. Most of the organization respond during the year-end audit, which is not a good practice.

Well-Defined roles & responsibilities (RACI) is important to emphasize teams on compliance and audit controls with a centralized dashboard, however, if people do not act on their responsibilities, it will be challenging. In our view, licenses management should be launched as an independent project with required. Unlike hardware asset management, it is complex to manage software assets due to the lack of end-to-end visibility of the products. Hence, this would result in a lot of time and efforts lost during the audit to provide a detailed review of the licenses to the audit team. This may be internal or external. With your internal audit team, there is a scope to improve, however with the external auditor, things could get complicated.

One of the daunting tasks of a license manager is to avoid repetitive mistakes in managing licenses inventory and avoid compliance issues. In one of the lawsuits filed by SAP against a major brewery due to non-compliance with the value up to $ 0.75 Mill USD. It is a pity that customer lost revenue, integrity and the stock value of the company went down drastically. I do not need to emphasize the consequences of non-compliance, especially if you're a public traded company, then there is every chance that customers will lose interest and they'd question your corporate integrity. Therefore, every organization should strive to start a robust licenses management practices with dedicated asset managers to manage the software licenses. It is essential to control, monitor with forecasts. In one of the cases studies, we had several challenges as highlighted below. Now, let's take a closer look at the pitfalls in software license agreements.

Editor Service Request management

Defect and Non-Defect Management

You can go online to submit Your incidents, check their status, manage Your support account and create a single view of all Your Service Requests and share it with everyone in Your company. This online service is available 24 hours per day, 7 days per week (subject to temporary unavailability for system maintenance).
Defect and Non-Defect Management does not include: enhancement requests and the development of in-depth methodologies (for example, detailed API consulting). Support for the development of customization and/or new applications using Licensed Programs may be arranged under a separate agreement (e.g. Developer Support offer). There are different types of support such as:

- Premium Support – 24X7 coverage with dedicated services support with customization benefits
- Basic support - Based on SLA's shared services model
- Pay-As-You-Go: For SaaS applications with charges based on the actual consumption

41

Maintenance Escalation Procedure

If You encounter a severe incident with Licensed Program, Your Service Request is raised to management-level attention, accelerating certification and resolution time according to the CRITSIT process as defined in section 5.4 hereunder.

8x5 Phone Support

The ADVANTAGE package allows You to access by phone a local «Support Center» (in English, except when local language support is available) from 9 am to 5 pm local time Monday through Friday (excluding major holidays, local time is defined as the time zone of the local «Support Center» providing support to You).

Optional Extended Support Phase Support Service

At the end of the Full Support Phase, within a period to be determined by editor specifically for each Release, you may extend your SECURE or ADVANTAGE Support Service, as applicable, subject to Your payment of all applicable charges. During the Extended Support Phase, the Service Request management is limited to the management of urgent Defects that are found in production and escalated via the CRITICAL escalation process.

Optional Sustaining Support Phase Support Service

At the end of the Extended Support Phase, within a period to be determined by DS specifically for each Release, you may extend your SECURE or ADVANTAGE Support Service, as applicable, subject to Your payment of all applicable charges. During the Sustaining Support Phase, the Service Request management is limited to Non-Defect management.

The Support Team is a worldwide multi-tiered organization, located in the Americas, Asia and Europe to help You meet Your reasonable expectations and provide You with responsive and proactive Support Service. When You contact the DS Support Team, a unique Service Request number is assigned to Your incident. This Service Request number is used for tracking the resolution process as it progresses. The Support Team will analyze the Service Request, and if possible, provide You with an applicable solution. However, when necessary, Service Request requiring more information than available at the first level of support will be transferred to the appropriate people within the editor company support organization.

The editor Support Team will make commercially reasonable efforts to address your Service Request based on its validated urgency level as follows. However, this does not constitute an obligation to correct or to solve any reported Service Requests as highlighted below with service level agreements (SLA):

Service Level Agreements (SLA):

Urgency Level	Initial Response Time
Urgent	**2 business hours**
High	**4 business hours**
Medium	**8 business hours**
Low	**2 business days**

Summary

In this chapter, you've studied common pitfalls of license non-compliance with examples of real-time case studies. These case studies reviewed would help you mitigate outstanding risks in your organization with requirements of SAP digital Licenses with the evolution of SAP licensing model with the emphasis on SAP License management practice. This would help you manage the compliance and audit requirements. Now, let's look at the holistic approach on accomplishing the ambitious digital licenses topic with case studies in the next chapter.

■ ■ ■

Chapter 3: License Management Methodology

The main objectives of this chapter are to discuss license management methodology with real-time case studies and compliance challenges. Now, let us examine a real-time case study with the SAP License compliance & audit requirements. Here is one of the real-time case studies where the client embarked on a journey to optimize the licenses count. However, the client was not sure where to start from, hence needed a baseline analysis to identify the current baseline licenses head-count prior to optimization of licenses.

The key objectives of this chapter:

1. Overall methodology
2. Identify the license types and optimize usage to reduce non-compliance with license reclassification
3. Metrics driven method to identify license compliance requirements
4. Identify the tools to finalize license position
5. Risk based approach
6. Best practices & recommendations

The key challenges are to find the current licenses baseline and then optimize to reduce non-compliance. This strategy can be used to benefit negotiations phase to procure additional licenses from respective publishers. However, the key point is to minimize risk of non-compliance, which may lead to penalties with legal implications. Based on the analysis, most of the companies do not have a strategy to manage licenses non-compliance or even measure what is there in the landscape.

This should one the key activities that must be on critical path to ensure risks are mitigated and the landscape is measured at regular intervals. Otherwise, you would end up paying licenses for everything installed without realizing the usage. The key part is to understand the non-compliance is to measure the current inventory with consumption analysis. This is what clients call it as a license dashboard where management teams will gain glimpse of procured quantity of licenses with consumption and the GAP. This gap is non-compliance part, which would be typically dealt across cross-functional teams.

In addition to the DIRECT licenses, INDIRECT licenses which refers to the users accessing core ERP from a third-party application may pose significant risks to the landscape and its users, since you cannot count batch process that access information from core ERP or even the mobile devices that sends multiple remote function calls (RFC) in a batch process. Therefore, identifying the list of users accessing from these third-party applications may remain a challenge. Each of these events triggering an information pull is essentially could be your breach of licenses contracts, unless it is clearly specified. Let us analyze detailed phases in the license management methodology as illustrated below.

License Methodology

Phase I - License & Financial Analysis	Phase II - Strategy & Planning	Phase III - Negotiation Cycle	Phase IV - Contract Maintenance
Assets & Entitlement analysis Questionaire & Interviews GAP analysis & reconciliation report Strategic roadmap & forecast Financial analysis	Benchmarking Risk analysis Negotiation scorecard Communication plan	Financial & Business requirements Propsoal analysis Legal Terms & Contracts reviews Final agreement review	Post negotiation review Benefits analysis Communication plan Annual review

Phase (I): License & Financial Analysis

The Software Licensing Service and Financial Analysis phase involve assessing your current licensing assets and forecasting your future technology needs based on how your company may evolve in the coming years.

The process for Phase One includes:

a. Consolidated asset management and Licensing Reconciliation: This process sets the stage for everything that comes next and involves gathering in-depth data to determine your actual software assets and how they are currently being used. SAM team will provide an extensive physical and conceptual guideline for how this data should be collected, to achieve maximum accuracy and efficiency. Your internal questionnaire and customer interviews help you fine-tune the data, so you will know exactly the installed software you have versus purchased assets.

This also lays the groundwork for the creation of an internal, strategic roadmap of vendor-specific requirements. Using this data, it is possible to generate a comprehensive Reconciliation Report which translates the dry facts and figures into an easily-understood format you can use for decision-making. You will also need analyse potential points of leverage for the upcoming negotiation phase.

    b.   Financial and Technology Forecast: Using all the information you have collected; your software asset management team will then create a financial analysis outlining the various licensing options available and the ramifications of each option over the next three to six years. With detailed forecast helps you bring to the table additional options that may not be presented by vendors in their initial proposal or during the negotiation process.

Licenses Approach Overview

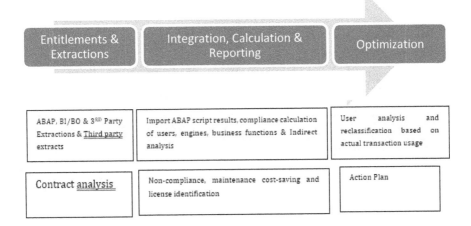

Entitlements & Extractions	Integration, Calculation & Reporting	Optimization
ABAP, BI/BO & 3RD Party Extractions & Third party extracts	Import ABAP script results, compliance calculation of users, engines, business functions & Indirect analysis	User analysis and reclassification based on actual transaction usage
Contract analysis	Non-compliance, maintenance cost-saving and license identification	Action Plan

SAP License Approach

As illustrated above with the detailed approach in the SAP Licenses Approach Overview, our goal is to evaluate current entitlements and extractions. To run standard SAP licenses transactions such as USMM to extract data from SAP landscape and de-duplicate using SLAW transaction in SAP Solution Manager (Solman) with various USMM output into consolidated report with exact licenses position. The above step would consolidate licenses mapped based on the assignment. However, the real challenge is to identify usage based on the transaction's usage. Hence, we developed ABAP scripts to analyse the report and recommend reclassifications of licenses, based on the profile and transaction usage.

This step is very critical during the audit procedures to determine the actual usage of the system by studying last 3 months of T-CODE (transaction), ST03N in productive environment for extracting active transactions utilized based on the history data.

Further, optimization is possible based on the above usage analysis of transactions, hence it is possible to determine the best licenses category for the users to avoid higher or lower licenses assigned.

Following licenses analysis steps illustrated below in Figure 1-3:

License analysis

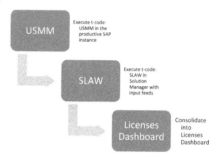

As illustrated above, we run USMM/SLAW transactions in SAP in sequence in the respective productive instances on a quarterly basis to gain good understanding of the licenses position at Client. The IT security team of Client executes these transaction codes, evaluate the current licenses position and re-classifies into appropriate licenses category based on the rule's setup. These rules identify the transactions usage based on last 3 months to study the t-codes used by users. These users are grouped into respective licenses category based on the real-time usage pattern of the system. This step would ensure Licenses compliance.

The Client IT team is responsible for developing an action plan to mitigate the risks of the above non-compliance or re-classification requirements as identified during the discovery step mentioned above. Post discovery step analysis, team would ensure appropriate discussions with functional and technical teams to ensure licenses policy adherence. Now, let us explore different category of licenses deployed at Client.

License Category

Broadly classified into following licenses category as illustrated below:

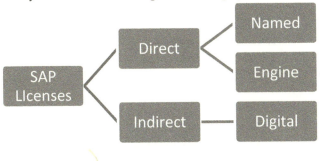

SAP Licensing

The main license metric for SAP applications is based on named users There are different varieties of 'named user' licenses for customers to purchase from SAP, including professional, limited professional, and employee. As we mentioned previously named users are attached to a username (based on any given date). This means that throughout the specific time you must not exceed the number of usernames that are defined within your SAP contract. Should a user leave the organization or change roles, which means they require using a different aspect within SAP, the license type can be changed.

It is important to remember that whilst SAP is procuring several organizations that create their own applications, the original applications licensing format may stay the same, and will not be moved to the SAP named user licensing structure.

Basic License Types

There are three basic license types for SAP applications. They are as follows:

- Professional User = named user who can perform certain operational tasks such as system administration or system management type roles that are within the agreed license metrics. The user should also have the rights that are specified by the SAP Application Limited Professional User.

- Limited Professional User = named user who can perform limited operational roles as defined by the software license.

- Employee User = named user who can perform tasks purely for the individuals own use and not on behalf of anyone else, task that are set out by the software license.

49

SAP ERP licenses rights on SAP GUI are measured through three different methods:

1. USMM
2. Accessed transactions
3. Used transactions

Key Challenges:

One of the key challenges in identifying the right license type is based on the profile. Unless your organization is well structured with proper assignment of licenses based on the activity profile. However, if the profile mapping is not done properly, then the alternate approach is to assign a default license category and then complete right assignment by analysing workload monitor based on the transactional usage.

Special License Types

Special license types can be defined by your organization. This form of license isn't considered 'official' as it is created by your local SAP Office, rather than SAP itself. There is no support documentation for this type of SAP license. Organizations need to clearly define what the parameters are for the special license types to ensure all users understand what they are licensed for. This also helps should an organization need more licenses, as they then know exactly what license type they require.

Being 'Audit Ready'

Unfortunately, SAP audits are quite a common occurrence, with most SAP users being audited in the past few years. There are several steps the SAP license managers can take to ensure that their organization is best prepared for any SAP audits. The first step is classifying your SAP users.

ERP Named Users

Classifying SAP Users

Determining the correct classification for SAP users is a tough challenge for any organization. There are several issues that we've touched upon, such as a user using different usernames for different SAP systems (example: Business Intelligence (BI) system for managerial reports, (2) an Enterprise Resource Planning (ERP) system for stock transfer reports, and, (3) a second ERP system for monthly invoice approvals). What level of SAP license should a user like that have? It's a question that any organization using SAP needs to find the answer to.

SAP does not supply a tool to classify users according to their activity. SAP does supply a standard SAP program (SAP transaction program) to collect any classifications that the organization has previously defined in all its systems and sends them directly to SAP for analysis and confirmation of its data.

There are two main issues when assigning SAP licenses internally. Both the cost of the licenses and the size of the organizations involved play a big factor in SAP licensing. The cost difference between a Professional User license type and an Employee license type is quite significant. This then forces the organization to think twice before assigning a higher-level license.

SAP users then also must think about how many SAP users they will need over the next few years (or over the term of the contract). What happens to those users that leave, or those users that change roles within the organization? It's an added complication to SAP licensing that must be considered, which is why organizations try and create simple, yet effective methods for classifying their SAP users. They must keep within the definitions set out by their SAP contracts however, so if they abide by the contract organizations can create any form of informal method for classifying SAP users. If they classify users accurately.

It is also worth mentioning that you will need to match up users with their usernames. It is vitally important to link all a user's usernames to their individual user account, so you can correctly identify what type of license the user needs.

Over time, SAP customers have created several methods for managing their SAP licenses, which we discuss below.

SAP Users by Usage

There are several elements to consider when classifying SAP users by usage:

Amount of activity

    a.   Identifying users by the amount of activity is probably the best way of assigning SAP license types. The more the user uses SAP or applications within SAP, then the higher 'level' of license type they require. As stated in our previous chapter, SAP activity is monitored by:

    b.   "'Dialog Steps", which, in practical terms, are the number of keystrokes and screens that are used. You can see these counts, for example, in SAP Activity ST03N (Workload Statistics). Using this method, the customer pre-sets a scale. For example, for users whose activity is up to 1,000 dialog steps per month, their license type will be set to "Employee"; for those with dialog steps totalling between 1,001 and 5,000, their license type will be set to "Limited Professional", and so forth. The scale can be set for an entire year, as a monthly average, or as a monthly maximum (i.e., the maximum value for all months in the last year)."

However, for users that have multiple usernames that each accesses a different system within SAP, the best license to assign for that user would be the highest value license so that the user is covered for all scenarios.

-The number of different activities

You can also identify users based on the different number of activities they access. This method of classifying SAP users can be unique to each organization, as they must specify and set parameters for how many different activities require 'higher' license types. For example, a user could use three different activities per month. Now that may be considered not a lot, so the organization would categorize them as having an 'Employee' license. The organization could then go on to say that anything above ten activities warrants a 'Professional' license and that anyone in-between is assigned a 'Limited Professional' license.

Using this method is useful for working out which SAP licenses are required on a monthly or even yearly basis. This can help with licensing forecasts and budgets both from a requirement aspect and from a financial point of view. Again though, with SAP licensing it is important to remember that users may have multiple user names within the SAP systems, so when looking at assigning licenses based on activities consideration must be taken for each usernames activity.

Type of activity or activity group

Within the SAP world, this is classified as the best method to classify users as defined by the SAP definitions. This activity or activity group method identifies the license level by the activities performed by the user. More important or complex activities will obviously warrant the higher-level license. An example of this can be seen below, taken from our previous SAP guide:

"Professional users perform activities associated with monetary transfers, while Employee users would typically perform activities related to viewing reports. The Activity Group method requires a definition of groups, such as Create, Change, and Display. You can say, for example, that a user who uses activities from Group 'Display' will be classified as 'Employee' – while a user who uses activities from Group 'Change' will be classified as 'Limited Professional'".

This method is the most time consuming out of the three to carry out. Organizations need to remember to carry out further investigation if they chose to identify users using this method as they will need to view the different activities carried out by a single user/username to establish what license metric they require.

SAP Users by Authorizations

There is also the option of classifying SAP users by their authorizations. As stated in our previous SAP guide, organizations "consider considering the classification of their users according to their "static" authorizations. In effect, this means that if a user is authorized to perform certain activities, he will be classified accordingly, even if he has never actually performed these activities."

Classifying users based on this method is short-lived since it is based on the organization thinking that their users are using 100% of all their authorizations, when realistically they are probably using 10% or less. This method is clearly not the best way for identifying and classifying users, which in turn means it's not the best way to manage SAP licenses. Using the methods mentioned previously is far more effective.

SaaS user Authorizations (Supplier Reporting SaaS Tool)

User Type	Definition	Example
Full Access	Full access	Create, Update etc.
Light Access	Report user who can input data, view dashboard without any administration capabilities	Employee that does not required full functionality

On the flip side, customers do not gain flexibility of customization to the SaaS software, which is an advantage is some cases, those who're using standard functionalities. There are no upfront investments required if the SaaS meets all your business requirements, hence you would save investment costs in terms of hardware, software and installation charges. However, there may be additional premium paid for hosting application in secured Google (GCP), HANA cloud platform (HCP), Amazon (AWS) or Azure cloud operational environment depending on customer requirements.

Extracting data manual method

In case the SAP version is older than ECC5, please extract manually and for each MANDT the same tables than the ones extracted through ABAP script

- Run SE16 transactions
- Enter the table name: UST12 (for example)
- below example will extract all lines for which the OBJECT has a name less than M (everything below M)

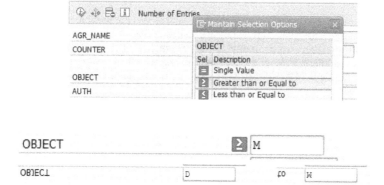

After having chunked part of the data, follow the steps below:

- Extract the output by clicking on « System », « List », « Save », « Local File » and choose « Unconverted »
- Export to the subfolder « Manual »

Host_SystemID_ApplicationType_ClientID_TableName_ChunkNumber.txt
Repeat for all chunk, all MANDT and both AGR_1251 and UST12

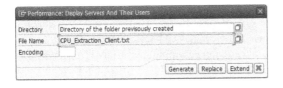

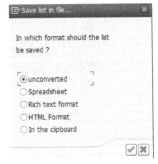

SAP Engine measurements

Software engines are an addition to the existing SAP licensing model. SAP engines are also known as SAP packages, and they are external components that are on offer to organizations should they need them. They are an additional cost and examples include the SAP Payroll engine. If the organization wants to process pays lips using SAP's Payroll system, then they will have to pay for that privilege outside of their license agreement. Each component has its own pricing and licensing model, so organizations will need to talk to SAP or their re-seller to ascertain what options their organization has.

Alerts need to be created for software engines so that the organization can see when they are nearing all their licenses being in use. This is important because without setting up alert's organizations could enter the non-compliant list. Setting up alerts helps manage existing licenses and provides an indication to the potential of reaching full capacity. For example, you have several Engines to assess scope of Indirect users creating, updating orders as illustrated below SAP Payment Engine as one of the core engines of SAP for payroll processing.

SAP Payroll Engine:

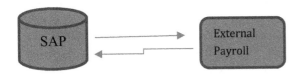

The above SAP Payment Engine (sample) is used for managing the PAYMENT outside of SAP such as 3rd party Payroll system or integration with PEOPLESOFT Payroll system. In the above illustration, SAP Payment Engine is used for managing the inputs channels via application programming interfaces (API), whereas the external system processes the payroll of employees maintained in SAP and returns control back to SAP for clearing and settlement to update the account payables.

Types of Engines:

- SAP Sales/Service Order
- SAP Purchase Order
- SAP Business Objects
- SAP Business Objects Financial Consolidation
- SAP Supplier collaboration
- SAP NetWeaver Process Integration (NW-PI)
- SAP Quality Centre (HP-QC)
- SAP Payroll processing (PY)
- SAP NetWeaver OpenHub (QlikView)
- SAP Work force performance Builder (WPB)
- SAP Application Integration framework
- SAP HANA Enterprise edition
- Database (Example. For access to Oracle Database)

An engine may be used for indirect access to core SAP ERP applications. For example, QlikView users can access SAP BW using NW Open Hub engine. A supplier can access core SAP ERP information from a third-party tool using SAP Supplier collaboration tool and HP-QC test center can access ERP data via SAP Quality center engine. The metric for each of these engines vary based on the block of users or CPU in case of Business Objects.

Engine access based on the USMM analysis.

- Execute USMM transaction and provide results on each productive and development systems.
- Results consolidated and imported using Data Analysis Tool
- All measurable engines as per the SAP marketplace will be analysed in the tool such as total orders created per year
- Measurable engine and relevant result (such as payroll)
  license compliance can be directly measured through USMM result
- Measurable engine and non-relevant result
  license compliance require specific inputs (declaratives, internal table extractions)

Exceptions:

1. The non-productive system BOXI QAS will not be measured. As a non-productive environment, the risk was qualified minimal.
2. BFC and GRC users will not be counted for the BO compliance.
3. The measurement of some engines is dependent on the reliability of the self-declaratives that were given. The concerned engines are:
   o SAP Supplier Collaboration
   o SAP Doc Access by open text
   o SAP Extended Manufacturing for Mill
   o SAP Product structure synch
   o SAP NW Process Integration
   o Database Interface

SAP Business Objects Measurements

- LMBI tools is provided by SAP to their customers and comes in two forms: data collection tool and data consolidation tool.
- LMBI Data Collection Tool execution has been requested.
- LMBI results for each system have been provided.
  The SAP BI Package product is mandatory to use products from the package. The BI Package product is licensed with named user licenses and CPU licenses.
- LMBI results consist of information such as Username, Feature accessed.
- LMBI results have been crunched with the official LMBI consolidation tool and following the official licensing rules (see here):
  This document indicates which product must be licensed for Dev/Test environment.

Exceptions:

1. BI User named user license and the BI Package license are not mandatory in Dev/Test Environment
2. Users have been deduped inside the tool based on Use rid, Mail and Full Name
3. License and Users have been consolidated based on license level (highest license level retained) and deduped user ID. Manual deduping have been performed to avoid some multiple counting for a single physical person

Phase (II): License Strategy and Planning

The Strategy and Planning Phase involves defining the optimal strategy to be used in the negotiation phase to come. The goal of this phase is to completely prepare your team for the negotiation phase. The stages in this phase include:

a. **Benchmarking**: As part of the strategy for your software licensing service, we perform in-depth competitive Benchmarking Analytics based on the priceless data we have curated from a variety of sources, including past agreements we have helped negotiate.

b. A comprehensive dashboard that maps your expected customer engagements with major software vendors, balanced against agreements that other corporations of similar size and with similar product-specific requirements have negotiated.

The purpose of this phase is to remove the sense of isolation that often occurs during the negotiation process. Corporations are often told their needs are unique and therefore difficult to compare to other customer agreements.

c. Negotiation Readiness and Strategy: It's important to prepare comprehensive readiness document which defines the software licensing strategies and stages that are critical to the success of the final negotiation. The Readiness and Strategy document provides not only expected negotiation strategy, but vendors expected responses. It details the goals of each side and the anticipated tactics of each. Its goal is to further demystify the negotiation process so that your negotiation team fully understands what you can expect from the negotiations. During this stage, we:

    a. Outline the different stages of the negotiation.
    b. Define the strategy and tactics to be used by the negotiation teams.
    c. Set the goals and budget criteria.
    d. Recommend participants in the negotiation team and fall-back alternatives.
    e. Detail objectives and planned strategy to further prepare the negotiation team.

Risk based Analysis

Identify applications that are subject to one of those risk mentioned below:
- **Risk 1**: Indirect applications with more than 200 users identified internally (risk is coming from SAP knowledge of applications connected to SAP systems and collected during migration, support,)

- **Risk 2**: Indirect applications with write/modify right from non-SAP user.

Applications in one of those categories were not included in the scope:
- Category 1: Read-only and asynchronous indirect application (Free of charge)
- Category 2: Indirect application with less than 200 users identified (Low risk)
- Category 3: Indirect application covered by an engine metric

Digital access is an outcome-based approach by analyzing documents created in SAP by the 3rd party, which is currently not clear and need clarifications from SAP measurement criteria.

Main Steps to assess Compliance

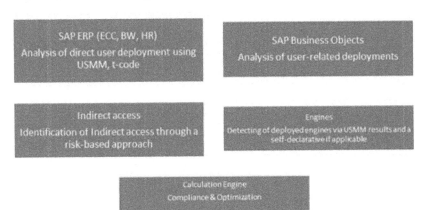

- **Stream 1: ensure managed SAP License compliance**

  - Evaluate monthly, the named user compliance

- Evaluate on a semester basis, the indirect accesses and engines deployments

- **Stream 2: implement process and tools through a managed service**

  - Implement USMM classification process (optimize license position with defined rules)

  - Implement Provisioning process (optimize license position with defined creation and deletion rules)

  - Implement Audit process (how to react when faced to an audit)

  - Customize the classification tool (define new ways of optimizations such as usage frequency)

- **Stream 3: in-sourcing program**

  - Take ownership of the knowledge and the tools

  - Build an in-sourced strategy (trainings, skills strategy, budget and effort planning)

  - Out-sourced License Desk to accompany Client when having specific questions

Phase (III): License Contract Analysis

For even the best-prepared team, the software license Negotiation Phase is the most critical and challenging. Your negotiation team enters this phase with a carefully and systematically developed plan designed by our licensing experts.

Typically, vendors will reply with a proposal. At this point, the frontal negotiation process begins and may go through several iterations and multiple interactions. You will need to assess your current license position with negotiation proposal to craft a response. Your asset team will need to interact closely with your negotiation team and company executives throughout this intensive process, sharing pointers and briefings, and generating response guidance.

You may end-up in iterations of the proposed agreement, analyzing the latest offering. By monitoring and helping to guide the software license negotiation process, software asset management team can protect your IT team from any attempts to delegitimize your decisions in favor of a speedy and all-too-often poor outcome. You will be prepared if approaches your executives to hurry the process along; in such a case we work to ensure that your company does not accept an unreasonable or lower-than-expected offer.

Contract Analysis

The SAP contract should be treated as any other software agreement or contract. Organizations can negotiate with SAP to get the best deal for their organization; so, don't be afraid to negotiate. There are several times or situations that are the perfect opportunity for negotiating your SAP agreement;

- Before implementing and purchasing SAP
- If you need to purchase additional licenses
- During a merger or acquisition

If you need to re-negotiate your SAP contract, those are the times to do so. Remember, SAP wants your organizations custom, so make sure you get the best deal for you.

Getting the Most Out of SAP Licenses

Getting the most out of SAP licenses is a tough challenge. Due to the licensing structure and the procurement process for SAP licenses, most enterprise (large) organizations purchase their licenses with the next few years in mind. They plan. To help optimize SAP licenses, enough tool needs to be in place to help identify what SAP users they have, and what aspects of SAP they are using. This will help the overall management of SAP licenses and will also ensure overspend on SAP licensing doesn't occur.

Furthermore, it is also important to have sophisticated and mature processes in place to manage the tool and SAP licenses. Said processes should already be in place for any organization with a SAM or License Management structure already in place, but SAP processes will need to be specific for managing SAP licenses due to its complexities.

Difference between most common SAP User License types

1. SAP Application Professional- With this license, user can perform Functional Operations and System Administration both. It is a full license. You can use any transaction, no matter if it's created, change or display. The Professional License gives the user full access whether required or not. It includes Users like who performs operational-related roles supported by the SAP software, who performs system administration tasks for the purpose of managing the performance of the application and maintenance of the latest revision level, who performs any human resources task, including but not limited to administration, payroll, time management, personal development, recruitment, total reward, training, strategic alignment and workforce analysis personnel within the customer organization (such as payroll administrators, recruiter, etc.), or External or internal consultants with customizing tasks.

   "Professional Licenses" is a full License for users, who can perform all activities.

   Example. System Administration (BASIS), Functional Consultants

   In most of the organizations limited or Employee usage may be the highest in number based on the role and the nature of the transactions used. In a logical way, you would be able to segregate usage into PRO: LPRO: EMP in the following ratio: 40:30:30. In other words, 40% pro, 30% limited and 30% limited may exist in the normal way, however usage must be carefully evaluated based on real-time transaction usage (ST03) and ensure you're able to realign the licenses assignment. This is very critical to ensure right amount of license consumption to avoid over paying publishers. You need to understand publisher's roadmap to leverage the benefits in the long-run. For example, SAP has revamped its indirect usage as mentioned below. This is a good opportunity for corporates to negotiate and get the best deal.

SAP License Model Revamped

Due to the increase in Digital Business and Transformation, SAP recently revamped its Licensing model to bring in more transparency for customers to help them consume and use the SAP applications optimally and to reduce the anxiety levels around the issue of SAP indirect access.

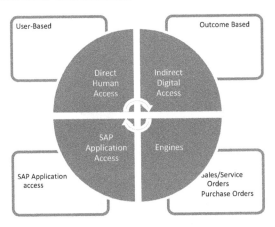

It majorly classifies itself in – **Direct** Access / **Indirect** Access

1. ***Direct*** (Named User / Package / Database) License – This has been the traditional licensing model followed by the customer's so far. With the shift from SAP ECC to SAP S/4 HANA there has been an impact of functionality wise purchase of licenses (Packaged License – priced by business metrics). The functionalities which were directly available in SAP ERP system (some post activation) are not completely accessible in S/4HANA. Hence, we now must understand it in more detail the implications and different options of purchasing the various SAP licenses required for the Business.

2. *SAP S/4HANA Simplification List gives you a basic understanding on License impact, egg – SAP S/4HANA leverages MDG-S for supplier distribution. The MDG-S license is not part of the SAP S/4HANA license.*

3. ***Indirect*** License – SAP systems data accessed via IoT, 3rd party applications or other digital access based on transactions/documents processed by the system itself. SAP identified nine document types that represent system generated records of commonly valued business outcomes from the Digital Core which will be part of the license, for any other document types there shall be no additional charge

Phase (IV): License Contract Maintenance

In other words, the renewal of the Enterprise Agreement is only the first step in securing your software licensing contract. Over the next three years, you will need to make several decisions and investment, how to utilize the technology assets you have acquired through the Enterprise Agreement, decide on how best to utilize the Software Assurance Benefits and prepare for annual True Ups. While renewing your contract with SAP, there are lots of factors that you'd need to consider such as the following:

    A.   Status Quo
    B.   License Exchange
    C.   Contract Conversion

Each of the above options may be viable for a client depending on the I.T roadmap planned as illustrated below:

Status Quo - Do Nothing	License Exchange	Contract Conversion
Solutions User License Direct, Indirect Named	Direct Pro, Light Pro, Emp Indirect Outcome based Digital	S/4HANA User License Outcome based

License Contract renewal

Status Quo – Do Nothing

This option is valid for the customers who do not want to change with the current license model. Depending on the situation client may not necessarily take any immediate action. For example, in our case study, our client did not have any compelling reason for almost a year to migrate to S/4HANA or any other license type. They were compliance in terms of Direct Named and the Indirect named licenses, however there could have been possible negotiations to save costs in the long run. The client decided not to take any action regarding the license swapping or negotiations.

License Exchange

This option is valid for customers, who want to exchange to the latest license model by exchange what they already have procured. For example. A customer may want to change from traditional to Direct Named Professional or Indirect/Digital categories from higher to lower and vice versa by utilizing the current contract. This would bring in more transparency and savings to the customer. You will be able to renegotiate your contract with SAP based on your roadmap. For example, in the case study discussed, our client exchanged some of the professional licenses to more quantity of employee license category. Secondly, due to the planned roadmap to migrate to SAP HANA for BW, most of the users were transferred to HANA license type. This would save costs and help you secure more licenses.

In addition, during the contract negotiations, is likely to have made concessions and included terms that are extremely valuable to your company. Let's understand different category of SAP Licenses and how we negotiate each of these license as illustrated below:

As per the new model **Document Licenses** is required when indirect access triggers the creation of certain sales or invoicing related documents.

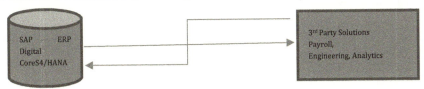

Contract Conversion

This option is valid for customers, who want to convert existing licenses to S/4HANA to utilize the latest model and transparency. SAP also separated License Sales from Audit and Compliance which will help the customers to separate their ongoing SAP usage commercials with the new requirements (i.e. new software package purchase). You have the option to convert named licenses in to SaaS or upgrade to S/4HANA licenses depending on your I.T roadmap or Indirect Named to Outcome based to avoid overpaying for the Indirect usage. For example, Indirect consumption is assessed based on the order type created, updated by the 3rd party users.

There are certain License Audit Tools already available for use of the customers

Case Study – A Large Manufacturing client

The software license contract was not well understood by the client. The software user rights document was extensive with several rights mentioned with metrics for measurements under on-premises consumption model. However, the client team had not reviewed in entirety leading to several non-compliances.

With several mergers and acquisitions done, client had totally ignored the license best practices such as internal audit and compliance procedure as recommended by SAP. This was one of the reasons for the client to be non-compliance from licensing point of view. The I.T landscape was very complex with the core ERP used for critical manufacturing business process such as Engineering to Order (E2O), Procure to Pay (P2P), Order to Cash (O2C) scenarios. Hence, the production orders were triggered by the ERP systems via a third-party interface. The core functionalities such as Sales Orders, Purchase Orders were created in ERP with portals for suppliers, customers etc. This is a classic example of DIRECT and INDIRECT SAP usage. The external users triggering updates into ERP are the INDIRECT users and the NAMED users are DIRECT users with specific licenses procured for professional access.

On one side, using a risk-based approach, client requested all interface application owners to send the list of users who're accessing the core ERP system to identify usage. However, there was no specific extract of which users are creating or updating documents in ERP. Since, these updates are managed via remote functional calls (RFC) via batch run monthly, there was no log of exact number of external users triggering the orders creation. Hence the team requested interface application owners to consolidate a list of users with specific update profiles to core ERP. This was a major risk item with respect to INDIRECT usage in SAP.

Another challenge was specifically maintaining inventory of SAP users with right license assignments. For example, Client team assigned 'PROFESSIONAL' category of user for all new users. This was very embarrassing as the PROFESSIONAL category usage is 2x to 3x times costlier than the Limited Professional or Employee license category. Typically, clients will check the profile of the users to identify the right transactions mapped prior to assigning the higher category. However, in this case study, client set up DEFAUL license for all users to PROFESSIONAL and then re-classified based on the exact usage of transactions by measuring /work-load monitor (ST03) transaction (standard SAP t-code for transaction usage) to study the number of transactions run by the respective users and then security team re-classified the users from PROFESSIONAL to other categories such as Limited Professional or Employee category of the license types. For example, a procurement user may run procurement transactions MM01, MM02 etc. Hence, there was no need for professional access for these procurement users. The above case is true for Finance, Sourcing, supply chain and report users. There was no need to classify them under professional category.

Apparently, client lost the ability to negotiate with SAP more effectively in subsequent negotiation phase and they were on the back seat during the SAP audit. This situation could have led the customer to face legal consequences for non-compliance, if not addressed properly. Hence, there is a need for license dashboard used by software asset management (SAM) teams to ensure compliance at any given point of the year.

One of the best practices is to maintain accurate inventory of licenses in a dashboard with consumption till-date. In the above case study, client listed usage details based on actuals and re-classified on a quarterly basis. Instead of this approach, if you're able to assign profiles to the right license category and maintain the consumption rate, then it would be much simpler. Whenever SAP comes for an audit, they would request for lot of details as self-declarative for some products. The internal audit compliance procedure is a dauting task as it will need organization-wide collaboration across departments to ensure right information. Once automated it becomes an easy task to follow upon non-compliance by setting alert reminders. There are several tools available in the market such as Flexera that can help you manage a consistent dashboard or even QlikView for reporting. However, the point is to assess non-compliance by looking deeper at transactional usage to map the right licenses category. Hence, a deeper tool for transaction usage is required.

The client developed a batch extract from work-load monitor ST03 transaction on a quarterly basis to assess exact usage. Further the extract was fed into QlikView tool for analysing the patterns of usage such as procurement users using a set of transactions, which was further mapped in to right category of licenses by analysing the SAP contract. This approach helped client in identifying the right license category for users to map to the right licenses.

Transaction Table below illustrating sample mapping of transactions. (Reference only). This sort of table is required for every client based on your specific contract with SAP. The client is responsible for mapping the transactions to the respective process and the corresponding licenses category based on the specific contract with SAP.

Profile Mapping based on workload monitor

Process Name	Transactions
Display Transverse	All Display T-code
Purchase Request / Purchase Order Approval	ME54N / SO01 / SBWP / SWNWIEX / ME29N / ME54 / ME55 / ME35K / ME35L
Requester	ME51* / ME52* / MIGO / ML81N / MIGO_GR / MB01 / ML81 / MB1A / MB02 / MB1C
Non-Confirm (NCR)	QM*/IQ*
Work Order & Notification	IW32 / IW52 / IW41 / IW51 / IW31 / IW68 / IW58 / IW38 / IW8W / IW3D / IW72
Procurement	ME9F / ME21N
Time Booking	CAT2
Warehouse	LM01 / YYYLMXX / LM00 / LM03 / LM05 / LT11 / LM12 / LM58 / LM06 / LT01 / YYYLMYY / LT05 / LT31 / LX01 / LT15 / LT12 / LT04 / LT03 / LT10 / LT0G / LU04 / LL01

The above analysis would help you assign the right licenses category. Perhaps, you can automate a process to manage extract from core SAP and then upload into QlikView to analyse transactions based on the mapping maintained above. The compliance dashboard would help you assess degree of non-compliance on a quarterly basis.

As mentioned, client followed a risk-based approach for analyzing Indirect access, for example, there were few Engineering and sourcing application users creating, updating documents in ERP. Hence, these applications with large users updating ERP was identified. In this case study, Bill of Material (BOM) data was created by the external third-party Engineering users. Also, there were sourcing users created purchase orders in the ERP system triggered via supplier portal. These systems were identified and categorized as high, medium and low risk category.

Table illustrates the compliance Work package with description and deliverables

Work Package	Description	Deliverable	Suggested Frequency
ERP Named User compliance	Complete analysis with every BO system Include licenses required for SAP access Control and SAP Financial Consolidation users	Update of ERP Named User Effective License Position (Excel and Power point)	Monthly
BusinessObjects Compliance	Complete analysis with every BO system Include licenses required for SAP aces' Control and SAP Financial Consolidation users	Update of BO Effective License Position (Excel and Power point)	Monthly
Engine compliance	Analyze USMM data and self-declarations	Update of Engine Effective License Position	Quarterly
Indirect access compliance	Indirect Access Assessment based (update templates and declaratives)	Update of Indirect Users Effective License Position (Excel and Power point)	Quarterly
Custom Client Licensing Tool	Customize SAP licensing tool to adapt it to Client	Custom tool (ABAP and SQL	S1 2018

69

	environment and optimize efficiency and precision	scripts) Deployment guidelines Functional documentation	
Renewal negotiation	Expert team will support sourcing teams in manage license discussions with publisher		Annual

Table illustrates the list of tasks to execute for licenses analysis

Tasks	Description	Deliverable	Suggested Frequency
USMM Classification Process	Help set up a process to optimize user classification according to business needs	Classification Process	S1 2018
Provisioning Process	Help set up a process to optimize unused licenses usage and to homogenize best practices about creation/update/deactivation of user accounts	Provisioning Process	S2 2018
Audit Process	Help set up a process to guide Client behaviour in case of a license audit Share audit best practices	Audit Process	S2 2018
In-sourcing program	SAP licensing and audit knowledge Train on different tools and templates	Complete documentation Trainings	S2 2018
Licensing Desk	Answer to Client questions regarding licensing or tools	Licensing Desk	S2 2018
Service	Description	Deliverable	Suggested Frequency

Here is list of typical findings based on an internal audit compliance analysis as mentioned below.

Compliance & Audit Findings

Findings

Licensing Rules

1. Only licenses in productive systems and developer licenses are counted (only for Dialog users)

2. License 91 (Test) in productive systems are counted as Professional license

3. License 71 (unclassified) in productive systems are counted as Professional license

4. Only Dialog users are counted

USMM

1.   Client Transports has been requested to execute USMM transaction and provide results on each productive and development systems (for productive systems, only productive clients are to be measured)

2. Inactive users have been cleansed (all users with filed USR02.TRDAT >90D when extraction is performed)

3. Non SSCR registered administrators have been cleansed

4. LAW files have been consolidated through SLAW transaction (user basic deduping based on use rid)

5. Advanced deduping has been performed (based on full name, long mail or short mail) to avoid multiple licenses for a same physical person

6. Licenses have been reconsolidated based on the advanced deduping process

Transaction Usages

1. An ABAP script used to extract data from SAP system internal tables

2. ABAP script results containing tables regarding users and transaction usages

3. Data have been consolidated and imported in a Data Analysis Tool

4. Users have been deduped based on, by priority, Use rid/Long Mail/Short Mail/Full Name.
   Admin/Generic accounts have been excluded from deduping.

5. License classification have been made based on transaction usages

   - A dictionary has been maintained to map a license to each transaction

   - For each user, a consolidation has been made based on the transaction used (highest license)

6. USMM has been leveraged to identify developers

Indirect Access Audit compliance

SAP has various types of customers and corresponding licensing models. These include traditional SAP ERP (SAP ERP Central Component or SAP ECC) customers with the named user licensing model, SAP S/4HANA® customers without a named user model, and customers with both traditional SAP ERP and SAP S/4HANA, both under a named user licensing model.

The indirect access audit practice and approach described here and in the following sections specifically address indirect access of the core SAP ERP for traditional SAP ERP (SAP ECC) customers that have not licensed the "SAP digital access software engine." Individual contracts may include special agreements that deviate from the standard approach. In such cases, the process described by the decision tree below would not apply. To determine whether indirect access of the core SAP ERP software is within the customer's SAP ERP license level, SAP license auditors will normally follow the decision tree shown Figure 1.

SAP Auditors view of Indirect Access

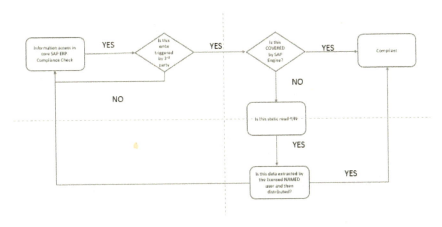

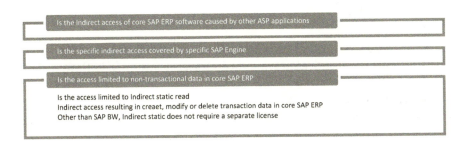

The above picture illustrates view of Indirect access by SAP Auditors. These are the key questions to ask from an Indirect access to your core SAP ERP perspective. It is important to understand these criteria for determining Indirect usage. For example, if your users are directly logging in to retrieve information in core SAP ERP, then these users will need Direct NAMED user access. As discussed earlier, your security team will assign the right entitlement (category of licenses) based on the profile, activity mapping. Now, if the user is accessing your core SAP ERP from a third-party application, then the user is classified in to INDIRECT access user, which could be a batch processing user for example, a remote function call (RFC) user who may trigger a batch process in SAP ERP or even a simple static read in core SAP ERP.

In either case, it is qualified as an Indirect access, hence you will need appropriate SAP Engine to enable indirect access to your core SAP ERP. For example, payroll processing may be done outside of SAP and post processing accounts payables are updated in core SAP ERP. This is a classic example of Indirect access with update. Hence, you will need to procure SAP PAYROLL engine to enable Indirect access from 3rd party payroll system. Similarly, orders engine enables indirect access for Sales/Service and Purchase Orders. SAP has further enabled outcome-based license model for measuring exact document types created by third party applications in SAP.

Summary

In this chapter, you've studied the importance Of License Methodology with approach described with case studies. This would help you plan your organization license program launch to access baseline and the best practices. There are various tools provided by SAP to accomplish compliance requirements as discussed through the chapter. This would help you manage the compliance and audit requirements.

References:

(License Audit Workbench / Measurement Program (transaction USMM) for measuring users and engines)
Licensing SAP Software – A Guide for Buyers
SAP Global License Audit and Compliance Update

Ref: service.sap.com/license auditing

Chapter 4: Compliance and Audit best practices

The main objectives of this chapter are to discuss compliance & audit best practices real-time case studies with compliance challenges. Mostly software Licenses is one topic that would bring the entire organization as one global team, regardless of the internal political situations, however at the same time, it imposes a lot of risks to the entire organization top-to the bottom. You must understand that there are huge penalties imposed by the vendor in case of non-compliance, thus leading to risking your core business operations, if not understood properly. Hence, it is a great responsibility for managers.

You'd realize if there is a non-compliance, everyone will be in the line of fire. If managed diligently, these issues could be averted to avoid a major financial loss with several lawsuits filed due to non-compliance. This was the case when SAP filed a lawsuit in one of the customer situations due to non-compliance with significant $ financial implication up-to $ 10Mill USD. The customer is one of the largest brewery company based in Europe with global operations. The core ERP was SAP with several interfaces. Some of these B2C portal users were able to create sales orders directly from the portal interface with a transaction triggered by the user via remote functional calls (RFC) to connect directly to SAP and create new orders. There were over 10,000 users with thousands or orders created every week.

Apparently, the above-identified situation resulted in several non-SAP users raising orders from the portal. Almost several thousands of orders were raised every month. Hence, in the claim, SAP had stated that the customer has used the software inappropriately and caused damages by accessing SAP data from a third-party portal without a proper SAP user accessing information in the system. Hence, there was a huge revenue loss incurred by SAP and they backdated usage of the B2C portal users and calculated over $10 Million USD as a penalty. Indeed, this was an alarming case study to realize the impact of the unethical practices conducted by the customer, knowingly or unknowingly. However, ignorance is not bliss in the case of contracts, courts, and judgments. I hope this situation does not occur in any of your customer cases.

The only way to avoid such issues is to be aware and discuss with respective audit teams, by setting robust audit practices backed up by software to monitor, control and optimize your usage. Let's understand the overall ITAM Governance structure.

IT Asset Management (ITAM) Governance

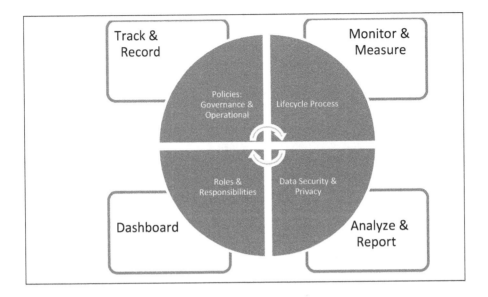

IT Asset Management (ITAM) is at the center of the core ITAM governance as illustrated above. There are five main work streams as part of the ITAM.

- Policies: Governance & Operational
- Lifecycle processes
- Data security and privacy
- Supporting Technologies &
- Roles & Responsibilities

We discussed the lifecycle of SAM core processes from asset procure to retire. As part of the overall ITAM governance, you should ensure operational process to manage the entire lifecycle.

Sequence of activities:

Task	Activity	Frequency	Team
ERP Direct usage – Technical	User logs into SAP and extracts data into excel for further functional analysis	Monthly	Technical
ERP Direct Reporting	Input ST03 raw data into Reporting tool	Monthly	Functional
ERP Direct usage – Functional	Analyze functional usage by respective transaction and map it corresponding Licenses category (Pro or Light Pro) etc.	Monthly	Functional
ERP Direct usage – Re-classify	Security team will review output from the functional step and re-classify current licenses	Monthly	Technical
ERP Direct usage – Dashboard review & update	Updated dashboard with current licenses position	Monthly	Software Asset Management
Indirect access	Ensure Engineering and Support functions teams update usage data in the repository SP folders created to understand the current Indirect position	Monthly	Indirect (Engineering/Support Functions)
Indirect access – Dashboard update	Ensure INDIRECT license position is updated	Monthly	Software Asset Management
BI Licenses Position	Analyze usage by CPU, Indirect users accessing BI information	Monthly	Support Team
Quarterly Audit Review	SAM team will execute quarterly audit review procedure to ensure alignment and a step towards the final audit prop	Quarterly	Asset Team
Yearly Audit review	Sourcing team will execute annual audit review procedure to ensure alignment to review audit step	Yearly	Sourcing/SAM
Contract review and	Discuss strategy to optimize licenses usage / additional	Yearly	LT/Sourcing/SAM

	procurement etc.		

The above tasks highlight the different types of licenses. It is important for respective teams to manage their tasks on a regular basis to keep the entire compliance check and audit controls. We have identified major pitfalls in managing digital licenses as highlighted below:

People-Process-Technology (PPT) Framework

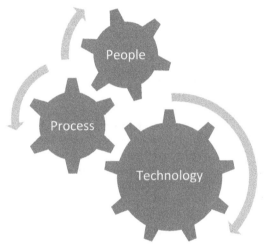

The above picture illustrates the PPT Framework with the core people, process and technology impacting the compliance. Let us explore the pitfalls listed below:

A. People:

1. Lack of dedicated leadership focus
2. Lack of dedicated workstreams focused on licenses products that they use daily
3. Lack of dedicated licenses practices team with defined RACI with stakeholders from Projects, Operations, Software Asset Management (SAM) and Admins to support respective tasks
4. Lack of knowledge on the entitlements linked to specific licenses terms and conditions

79

5. Lack of management focus on software assets leading to huge financial losses
6. Lack of consultations with internal legal, sourcing teams to ensure compliance

C. Process:

1. Lack of dedicated methods to implement best practices
2. Lack of quality check on licenses availability, forecasts to ensure compliance
3. Lack of internal audit controls, procedure to prepare teams for the final audit
4. Lack of risk assessment and control methods, thus leading to issues including financial losses.
5. Lack of control procedures for new users, user activation / de-activation policies implementation.

D. Technology:

1. Lack of complete licenses inventory of the software products & suites using a tool-based approach to measure usage with defined metrics
2. Lack of managing entitlements up-to-date
3. Lack of traceability of the software purchases against the Purchase Request, Purchase Order
4. Lack of visibility to the entitlements (contracts) managed with the respective software vendor
5. Lack of visibility to the amendments to contracts such as exchange offerings on specific product suites
6. Lack of legal awareness on licenses breach leading to significant penalties
7. Lack of sanctions imposed by the vendor
8. Lack of regular contact with the respective vendor account manager to assess the current licenses position
9. Lack of disclosure to avoid penalties may lead to legal issues and unethical behaviour
10. Lack of regular internal audit with well-defined workflows
11. Lack of dedicated resources may lead to poor inventory tracking
12. Lack of coordination between teams, leading to different data set information

Essentially, you should group licenses topics into the following:

1. **Compliance & Audit team** – Overall compliance officer is responsible for enforcing best practices. The Software Asset manager is responsible for respective assets inventory and forecast with regular audits to identify and mitigate risks involved.
2. **Inventory management** – Software Asset Manager (SAM) manager is responsible for managing licenses inventory and forecast regularly. It's important to connect internally between teams to provide a clear visibility regarding the status of licenses. The License manager is responsible for the status by connecting with all departments, such as delivery, support and sourcing teams for licenses forecasts
3. Current Position with Forecasts by Project Delivery and operational support I.T teams

Risks

If you'd consider outstanding risks highlighted below:

1. Huge risk to the business due to sanctions imposed by the software vendor
2. Losing meritocracy with the customers, share-holders
3. Legal issues due to non-compliance with the respective supplier
4. Lost time, efforts and money about the leadership efforts in mitigating risks due to non-compliance
5. IT teams will lose focus and try to provide data points to mitigate risks without much of streamlined process, which may lead to internal conflicts between I.T and business departments.

A well-defined responsibility matrix (RACI) with teams such as SAM, Project, Operations and the business are required to participate in the license program. It is important to emphasize teams on audit controls with a centralized dashboard, however if people do not act on their responsibilities, it will be challenging. In our view, licenses management should be launched as an independent project with required resources, as it may lead to enormous amount of time-spent in extracting data from productive instances to study the usage patterns. Unlike hardware asset management, it is complex to manage software assets due to lack of end-to-end visibility of the products. Hence, this would result in a lot of time and efforts lost during the audit to provide detailed review of the licenses to the audit team. This may be internal or external. With your internal audit team, there is a scope to improve, however with the external auditor, things could get complicated.

One of the daunting tasks of a license manager is to avoid repetitive mistakes in managing licenses inventory and avoid compliance issues. In one of the customer situations, SAP filed a law suit against a major brewery due to non-compliance as mentioned earlier. It is a pity that customer lost revenue, integrity and the stock value of the company went down drastically. I do not need to emphasize on the consequences of non-compliance, especially if you're a public traded company, then there is every chance than customers will lose interest and they'd question your corporate integrity. Therefore, every organization should strive to start a robust licenses management practices with dedicated asset managers to manage the software licenses. It is essential to control, monitor with forecasts. In one of the cases studies, we had several challenges as highlighted below.

Team Roles & Responsibilities

Team

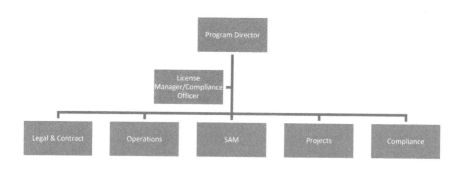

The above team charter illustrates a typical license governance team with various functions supporting the audit & compliance program. SAM holds the key for coordinating with different streams and conduct a monthly, quarterly reviews.

- Identify and record current assets.

- Maintain an up-to-date and accurate record of all IT assets required to deliver services and ensure alignment with configuration management and financial management.
- Manage critical assets. Identify assets that are critical in providing service capability and take steps to maximize their reliability and availability to support business needs.
- Manage the asset life cycle.
- Manage assets from procurement to disposal to ensure that assets are utilized as effectively and efficiently as possible and are accounted for and physically protected. Optimize asset costs. Regularly review the overall asset base to identify ways to optimize costs and maintain alignment with business needs.
- Manage licenses. Manage software licenses so that the optimal number of licenses is maintained to support business requirements and the number of licenses owned is enough to cover the installed software in use.

License Management project plan

Typically license project management has two phases which may run from 8-12 weeks with parallel tasks to complete the entire study. This would help your organization plan the licenses requirement, set up a dedicated software asset management practices to ensure 100% compliance to stay away from the last-minute hassles of license audit conducted by the respective publisher. Once you complete the study, it will be a recurring license dashboard maintenance activity.

Phase I License Due Diligence Phase

a. License Contract Analysis – Client team should diligently review the contract with their in-house legal, sourcing and IT teams to nail down every single point mentioned in the contract. The software user rights documents are very complicated from legal, sourcing and technical point of view. Hence, the entire team should read it multiple times before signing the contract.

b. System Usage Analysis – Typically, with SAP systems, standard transactions such as /ST03 is used to gauge the usage based on number of transactions hits for last 3 months. This survey would help them assess usage history with corresponding license entitlement.

c. Requirements Assessment – The primary deliverables of this phase are to assess 3-5 years of IT roadmap to ensure adequate licenses are planned with the technology shift or makeover anticipated.

d. Optimization – The objectives of this phase is to understand the baseline compliance position and draft a plan to achieve benchmark based on data collection and survey. For example. In the case study, we have observed lack of proper planning in license assignment, there by leading to highest category of licenses assigned to the users. This may lead to huge license deficit in higher category and increase the costs significantly. Hence, it is important to understand the optimization possibilities.

1. Building a robust licenses management dashboard accessible for the entire team
2. Compliance reporting on a regular basis
3. Audit process with key stakeholders involved
4. Ensure accurate inventory and forecasts using a tool-based approach
5. Finalize software management tools for reporting with a high-level dashboard view
6. Define tools, methods and process for licenses management
7. Industrialize licenses inventory stock control and forecasts based on the actual usage of the software
8. Define methods such as Pay for what you use
9. Define standards
10. Define appropriate optimization techniques to resolve complex interfaces
11. Define financials and ensure budgetary targets are met

License optimization

SAP license audits can be stressful events for organizations that aren't prepared. With the rising frequency of these audits and the budget issues they can cause, today is as good of time as ever to avoid a future headache and get your organization prepared.

Tool based license monitor

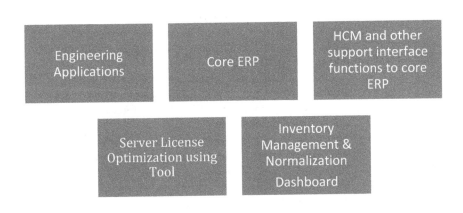

Tool based License monitor

- Drawing on our experience of helping organizations optimize their SAP license allocations in preparation for an SAP license audits, we've come up with seven steps that will not only ensure you're ready for your next license audit but also potentially save you millions in license costs and maintenance fees.
- Assess your current SAP license status
- The first step to preparing for an SAP license audit is knowing where you stand today. A proper assessment includes comparing your USMM and SLAW reports with your current license agreements, determining how well you understand indirect usage, and forecasting your consumption of user and engine licenses.
- Kick-off a two-week license management project – or not
- Once you know your current SAP license status, you can decide if a short project to improve license allocations is worthwhile. The goal of this two-week license project is to pull all your data together into one place and to determine if you can reduce compliance risks and expected costs through improved license allocations.

Assuming a two-week project makes sense, you should start by getting all the data you need into one place. For example, you should:

- Collect all SAP licensing contracts into one place and understand your total licensing envelope for users and packages.
- Identify all package or engine licensing metrics.
- Identify all applications integrated into your SAP environment and all the users for each one of the integrated applications.
- Get the most likely IT capacity forecast for the next 6-18 months. Ideally, you already have an IT capacity forecast that is based on your firm's business plans, but if you do not then you will need to get a copy of your firm's business plans and then translate that into an IT capacity plan.
- Once you have the above information, you can use it in the following steps to build a license forecast for SAP users and for SAP packages (a.k.a. engines). Your license forecast should answer three key questions:
- What SAP users will be added based on your business plan?
- What indirect users will be added based on your most likely business or IT capacity plan?
- How will your engine licensing metrics increase or decrease due to the business activity levels implied by the business plan or IT capacity plan?
- Build a forecast to anticipate direct user license requirements and define rules for optimally allocating direct user licenses.
- Once you have the necessary information in one place you can start using it. We recommend starting with understanding and optimizing your direct users since this is typically the least complex licensing area and much of the work done for direct users can be leveraged when managing compliance for indirect users. Start by:
- Analysing user transaction histories to identify and remove inactive and duplicate users.
- Defining an assignment ruleset for allocating license types to users based on what access they have.
- Running simulations to determine if there are enough licenses for direct users based on the most likely and most optimistic business plans.

These steps can be difficult without a tool like our License Management module which captures detailed user transaction history, supports complex assignment rules, and offers simulation support. However, the rewards are significant once a company has optimized their license allocations and understands how many are truly consumed. Only then can companies maximize their investments in SAP by ensuring that users aren't assigned more expensive license types than they are using, and only then can a company understand how much spare capacity (headroom) they have and if those unused licenses are enough to meet the near-term requirements implied by the current business plan.

- Optimize indirect user licenses
- Optimizing licenses for indirect user access is perhaps the most challenging license management tasks. Begin by building on the work done in step 3. Take the rules you've created for assigning license types to your SAP users and use them to determine how each of the roles for each user of each "non-SAP" application would map to an SAP license type. To do this, simply ask yourself, "If the user were to read or change data in SAP directly instead of through the integrated application, what roles would they need and what license type that would require?"

Once you have mapped SAP license types to the application roles in the "non-SAP" application then simply compare the list of direct SAP users along with their assigned SAP license type with those users of the "non-SAP" application. Once you have compared the two lists, ensure that every user with both an SAP user ID and access to the "non-SAP" application has an SAP license type assigned to them that is equal to or greater than what they would require due to their access to SAP through the third-party application. And, for those who only have indirect access, ensure the SAP license required of them due to their access levels in the third-party application is accounted for.

- To optimize indirect user licenses, it may be necessary to create or modify role definitions in the third-party application or your SAP license assignment rules. Here again, leverage the work done in step 3. Also important is to use simulations based on your current IT capacity plans and business plans to see how the planned usage of the "non-SAP" application might impact licensing. Check your simulation results against your existing license inventory and see how long your company can go before needing to purchase additional licenses.
- Understand current consumption levels of package or engine licensing metrics
- While optimization of licenses is most often done at the user level, if you want to easily pass your SAP license audit you will need to ensure you understand the consumption of licenses associated with owning a given software package. These metrics vary widely. Not only are they different from one product to the next, but they can also differ from one version of the product to the next. Be sure to review what metrics are in your contracts and how those metrics are expected to change based on the business plan and IT capacity plans.

To make licensing audits stress-free, you will want to keep everyone informed on when incremental license purchases are expected. We recommend updating everyone monthly even when there is no need for more purchases, because this helps to remind people that if the business plan or IT capacity plan changes, then they will need to let you know.

- Monitor user and business activities, user count, and rates of change and then adjust allocations automatically
- At the end of your two-week license management project you will have assessed your SAP license status, gathered the required data, optimized your license allocations for both direct and indirect license allocations, and tentatively budgeted for any incremental licenses for users or SAP packages. Now is the time to put a simple process in place to ensure you stay ready for a license audit.
- Acquire additional licenses if needed

There comes a time, as your business grows and grows when you will need to buy more licenses – even if you have perfectly optimized your current investments. However, by using all the information you've gathered and the proficiency you've developed by continuously applying the above steps, you can now make informed decisions and any additional investments in SAP licenses will be just the right amount (not too much and not too little) and at just the right time (not too early and not too late). Furthermore, your purchasing decisions will be based on actual usage and aligned with expected business growth.

License Audit principles

SAP STANDARD AUDIT PROCEDURES

- The IT audit team will harmonize the end-to-end audit processes globally, from nomination to delivery of the license audit report by defining the scope, process, and results of the audit every 2 months.
- License Audit Scope Audits will be comprehensively outlined and communicated in advance to the technical and functional teams within Client. In general, Client performs basic audits and enhanced audits. Basic audits cover self-declarations and automatic measurements that customers perform. As such, the scope is limited to the information the teams provide, and most often they do not cover all licensed SAP products. However, Client Licenses PMO retains the right to request additional

information or to expand the audit when specific indicators have been discovered within the defined scope.

- For license compliance audits in which SAP believes findings show a significant issue, SAP may engage one of its auditors from another region to verify audit results. This would occur before the report is issued to the customer and would improve the consistency and quality of the audit results.
- Enhanced audits start with a clear statement of scope. On-site audits begin with a kick-off meeting, during which the audit's scope is communicated. License Audit
- The Client SAP Global License Audit and Compliance team will create a report for every license audit performed, and the license compliance team will be responsible for informing the customer of the report's availability.

In some cases, a license overuse may be identified without the performance of a license audit if required information verifying license compliance is publicly available. An example is product use based on the number of employees disclosed in a company's publicly available annual report. If the Client SAP Global License Audit and Compliance organization is involved in such a case, a report will be issued, shared, and discussed with the respective team(s).

License Self-Measurement

To reduce the risk of an unexpected license gap, SAP wants to make it easier for customers to monitor their license compliance themselves.

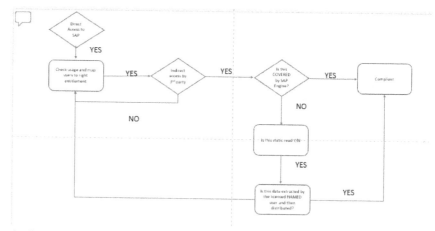

As illustrated in the above flow to check the direct and indirect access:

If the users are directly accessing your core SAP ERP, then the users can be classified based on the license entitlements as discussed earlier. This would determine your license costs based on assignments. These assignments are done by your internal security teams based on the user activity profile during used provisioning and monitored periodically. However, for indirect access, a lot of due-diligence is required to understand the usage such as read, write, modify transaction data etc. The following audit review points for your quick reference:

1. License audit workbench (LAW) tool is primarily used for basic audits. This tool is available free of costs for all SAP ERP users to review and monitor usage.

2. If your users are accessing directly as NAMED users, then point. 1, using LAW tool, you will be able to identify and extract usage details, however if your core SAP ERP is accessed via remote function calls (RFC) or a batch process, this needs to be licenses appropriately. A license auditor will first determine if SAP software is "used," as any use of the SAP software requires an appropriate license. "Use" is defined in SAP's current standard contractual documents as: "to activate the processing capabilities of the software, load, execute, access, employ the software, or display information resulting from such capabilities.

3. There are many misconceptions regarding licensing required for indirect access of SAP ERP. Clarification of the most common misconceptions are listed below: One-way or two-way: Regardless of

whether a user performs read-only, write-only, or read and-write transactions, all such transactions are considered use, and the user must be licensed as a named user.

For example. Real-time or batch transactions may activate processing in the core SAP ERP system, which needs to be licensed appropriately.

4. Users who access the SAP ERP system through one or more intermediary systems must be licensed.

5. Use of the SAP ERP system is independent of the technical setup (for example, SAP enterprise services, SAP Web services, BAPI® programming interfaces, RFC, Idec's, ABAP® programming language code, user exits, database link, file interface). No matter which interface is used to activate processes in SAP ERP, the user needs to be properly licensed.

6. If a user is accessing SAP ERP through a third-party application (for example, Salesforce or Workday) or through a custom front-end application that triggers SAP ERP processing, the user must be properly licensed.

7. Indirect static read is an exception to many of the above examples.

8. Upon the determination of "use" of SAP software, the auditor will verify the following decision node: ▯

    Does the use occur directly by individuals or indirect? The above definition of use from SAP's standard contractual documents covers both direct and indirect access. As this document concerns verification of indirect activities, it will focus on indirect use of SAP ERP (indirect access is a type of indirect use). Indirect access of SAP ERP typically occurs by way of a non-SAP front end, by non-SAP intermediary software, or through Internet of Things (IoT) devices.

9. Use of SAP ERP through direct access by an individual does require a named user license. If such use occurred by indirect access, the auditor will verify the next decision node:

Indirect access Checklist

Is the indirect access of SAP ERP initiated by other SAP applications?

Core business process (Indirect access) to SAP Engine mapping:

Core business process	Process	SAP Engine Required
Procure to Pay (P2P)	Create, Modify Sales Orders in core SAP ERP from 3rd party	Purchase Order Engine
Order to Cash (O2C)	Create, Modify Purchase Orders in core SAP ERP from 3rd party	Sales Order Engine
Customer's Employee views reporting such as financial statements in a non-SAP system, where such data was transmitted from SAP BW	Viewing SAP ERP data in non-SAP system such as portal	NW OpenHub or Named user license
IoT places orders directly in core SAP ERP	Create, modify orders by IoT	Sales & Services order engine
Shop floor transactions	User entering data in to core SAP ERP from a warehouse application, which is non-SAP system	Named user access
Customers distributor sends orders to SAP ERP via EDI	Orders report	Sales & Services order engine
Services	Create, Modify Service Orders	Service Order Engine
Payroll (HCM)	Run payroll and update core SAP ERP	Payroll Engine
Engineering	Conversion of manufacturing mBOM	

	to SAP BOM structure from 3rd party. Run Bill of Material (BOM) requirements planning in non-SAP and update core SAP ERP	
Material requirements planning (MRP) / Production Orders	Manage MRP external to core SAP and update to keep it in sync. Create Production orders in core SAP ERP and manage via shop-floor applications to update production order status	
SAP ERP sends purchase order to customer's vendor system for processing		Sales & Services Order Engine
Data extract from SAP ERP for dashboard		SAP NetWeaver OpenHub engine.
Customer uses PI to integrate non-SAP CRM system		Customer must license PI

1. Depending on the customer's license model, when indirect access of SAP ERP occurs from other SAP applications, such use of SAP ERP may be included in the SAP application license, regardless of whether the application is in the cloud or on premise. Examples of using SAP ERP through other SAP applications are:
    A. Purchase orders generated in SAP ERP by an SAP Ariba® solution
    B. Sales orders in SAP ERP modified through the SAP Customer Relationship Management application
2. When this type of indirect access of SAP ERP is covered by the license of the SAP applications, it does not count against the license level for SAP ERP. However, if the indirect access is not caused by such other SAP applications, the auditor will verify the next decision node:

3. Is the indirect access right covered by specific SAP software engines?

Some SAP software engines are designed for simplified licensing of specific indirect access, especially in business-to-business (B2B) and business-to-consumer (B2C) activities.

4. Examples of such engines are:
   A. SAP Sales and Service Order Execution solution for use in B2B and B2C activities
   B. SAP Purchase Order Execution solution
   C. Note: Some engines, such as the SAP Budgeting and Planning for Public Sector application and the SAP Tax, Benefits, and Payment Processing for Public Sector

5. solution for SAP CRM, do not require named users. If the indirect access is not covered by another engine, the auditor will verify the next decision node as follows:
   A. Is the indirect access limited to non-transactional data? SAP's contractual use definition does not differentiate between data types. However, for core SAP ERP, the license auditor will follow a more limiting practice: Auditors review only cases of indirect access that result in the reading, creation, modification, or deletion of transactional data in core SAP ERP. Indirect access that does not result in the reading, creation, modification, or deletion of transactional data in SAP ERP will not be counted against the license metric for SAP ERP.

6. Document Type Description Sales Orders Creation of business documents for the sales of goods and services within SAP® software. These can be created, changed, or viewed through electronic data interchange (EDI), external non-SAP applications, and other means. Such documents may include sales quotations, sales and service contracts, sales orders, and returns. Customer or supplier invoice Invoices are documents that indicate the material and/or service being billed, including, but not limited to, reading (automated import) supplier invoices into SAP software, or creating and sending invoices to customers from SAP software.

7. Purchase order Creation of procurement documents for goods or services that are loaded into an SAP software system. Such documents can be created, changed, and viewed through various interfaces and can include purchase requisitions, purchase orders, purchasing contracts, and confirmations. Service order or maintenance order

Service and maintenance documents created within SAP software for the management of work to be performed.

A. These can be created approved, adjusted, or viewed through external non-SAP applications by the service team. Production order Creation within the SAP software of production documents that indicate production related details associated with the manufacturing of a material (for example, type, quantity, and colour of a material to produce and when to produce it). These can be created, changed, or viewed through, for example, EDI or external non-SAP applications. Quality notification Creation of quality-related documents for machines and tools that are loaded into an SAP software system. A quality notification can include the details of a nonconformance (for example, an independent defect).

8. These can be created, changed, viewed, approved, or rejected through third-party applications or other non-SAP products. Material documents (goods movement) Creation of material documents for the movement of goods. The documents usually indicate specific material received, issued, or transferred to, from, or within a storage location or plant. Travel expense claim Creation of travel expense claim for reimbursement of accrued expenses that are loaded into an SAP software system. Such documents can be created, changed, approved, and viewed through various interfaces.

A. The audit practice for differing treatments of indirect access to various types of data, as specifically described in this document, is not and will not be reflected in customer contracts, as it is only a practice. SAP has a transactional data-based approach for indirect access, which may be reflected in a customer's contract if the customer licenses a new SAP digital access software engine. The SAP digital access software engine differs from the transactional data audit practice described in this document and likely would be preferred by most customers.

9. If the indirect access results in the creation, modification, or deletion of transactional data in SAP ERP, the auditor will verify the next decision node:

10. Is the use limited to indirect static read? Indirect static read is a scenario in which information has been exported from an SAP system (excluding the SAP Business Warehouse application or any third-party runtime database) to a non-SAP system pursuant to a predefined query that meets the criteria listed below. SAP's policy is that the use of such exported data in third-party non-SAP systems does not need to be licensed, if all the criteria listed below for indirect static read are met: The data was created by an individual licensed to use the SAP ERP system from which the information is being exported. It runs automatically on a scheduled basis. The use of such exported information by the non-SAP systems and their users does not result in any updates to or trigger any processing capabilities of the SAP ERP system.

11. This is the final node of the decision tree. It occurs after the auditor has verified all previous decision nodes. If the case in point is not limited to static read, the auditor will usually determine that the verified indirect access scenario requires a dedicated license.

Licensee Scenarios - Indirect

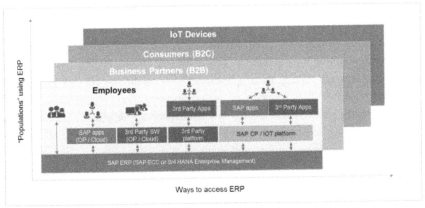

Ways to access ERP

Figure 1. ERP Use Scenarios

The above picture illustrated ERP usage scenarios. Indirect users may be your business partners, consumers, devices, automated systems, bots that use SAP ERP in addition to the Named users

You'll need to review your scenario of Indirect static reads in detail to identify indirect usage and finalize the usage and assess scope of changes in the new policy as illustrated below:

The new policy is schematically shown in Figure 3.

	A	B	C	D	E	F
Past policy	User	Included	User	User	Order	Not Defined
New policy for ECC	User	Included	User	Order	Order	Order
New policy for S/4*	User	Included	Order	Order	Order	Order

*Applies only for customers on the new model for S4 HANA Enterprise Management

97

As illustrated above as per new policy from SAP, ECC users can leverage the benefits of Order to Cash (O2C) or Procure to Pay (P2P) process. Any user who does a transaction in SAP as an Indirect user or Direct user can use the 'Order' based metric which is a consumption model, instead of a Name user model. For example. In ECC, if you have 10 users generating 1000 orders a month by Direct Named users and another volume of 1000 from Indirect access, then it is easy to convert them to the consumption based model by procuring O2C Orders Engine licenses say around 10k orders per month, then you'd not worry about the number of users as the engine license would measure the actual consumption of orders created, instead of tracking the users. This is an easy method to access your orders consumption model for optimizing licenses costs for both Direct/Indirect users.

In the newer licensing model, you have the following types:

a. Order to Cash
b. Procure to Pay
c. Indirect static read (For non Data analytics)

As stated above, P2P is very similar to O2C. however, in the case of Indirect static reads, you'll need to qualify exact data access from ERP as Indirect static read or not to consider for the Indirect licenses. Following table highlights Indirect static reads, example, you may extract finance data for tax and audit preparations. Or even run a payroll by accessing employee details in ERP. These are scenarios, where you'd need to pay closer attention to determine real Indirect access read or not. Upon confirmation, then you can quantify access. The indirect static read clause works differently for analytics.

Indirect Static Read Questionnaire (YES indicates an INDIRECT access) as listed below:

The below table illustrates license scenarios examples to provide general guidance on Indirect Static Read based on the Legacy Pricing Model.

Scenario	Example	Indirect Access (YES/NO)
An employee of SAP's customer views reports (e.g. financial statements, forecasts, etc.) in a non-SAP system, where such data was retrieved/ transmitted from the SAP ERP system, prior to the employee accessing it	Financial reports, forecasts	Yes

A licensed employee of SAP's customer downloads information from SAP ERP to a third-party software system, so others can view this information in the 3rd party software		Yes
An individual (not licensed to access SAP ERP) adds information to a predefined query, specifying an attribute to be included in such query, which was created by an individual licensed to access SAP ERP, which was set up to run on an automated, regular basis.	Report	NO
Customers of SAP's customer view a product catalog on a portal built on and operating on the SAP Cloud Platform, where product and pricing information originating from an SAP ERP and/or SAP S/4HANA system was transmitted to the portal prior to the individual accessing the portal		Yes
An employee of SAP's customer views his customer's master data in a table within a third-party application, where such information originated in SAP ERP and was downloaded to third-party application prior to the employee accessing it	External user accessing ERP data from a portal	Yes
An employee of SAP's customer views his customer's order status via third-party application, where such information originated in SAP ERP and was loaded from SAP in direct response to the employee's inquiry.	Master data	NO
A sales associate of SAP's customer checks inventory status in a custom-built inventory system, where such information originated in SAP ERP and was downloaded from SAP ERP in direct response to the inquiry		NO

An employee of SAP's customer accesses a third-party data analysis tool to sort, filter and analyze data that was transmitted from an SAP application prior to the employee accessing the third-party tool.		Yes
An employee of SAP's customer accesses a third-party data analysis tool to sort, filter, and analyses data that was transmitted from an SAP application prior to the employee accessing the third-party tool	Analytics using backend data from SAP ERP	NO
An employee of SAP's customer accesses a third-party application to sort data that was transferred from an SAP application prior to the employee accessing the third-party tool, and this employee subsequently initiates a transaction within the third-party application, which in turn triggers the updating of information in an SAP application	Creating a Purchas Order for example triggered by data from core SAP ERP	NO
A customer of SAP's customer or a sales associate of SAP's customer accesses a custom portal that is built on and operating on SAP Cloud Platform, where information such as product inventory or customer data, which originated in an SAP ERP system, was transmitted from SAP in direct response to the inquiry from such individual.		No
An employee of SAP's customer accesses a third-party application to view a report that has been downloaded from SAP Business Warehouse.	BI report usage	No
Data stored in the SAP system is transferred to a third-party planning and	Planning data access by third-	Yes

consolidation application prior to an employee viewing and processing the data in the third-party application.	party from core SAP ERP	
Data is aggregated and calculated in the SAP ERP system (for example, creation of a P&L, summary records per account) and transferred to a third-party planning and consolidation application prior to an employee viewing and processing the data in the third-party application.	P&L Financial reporting	Yes
Data stored in SAP ERP is transferred to a third-party planning and consolidation application, then it is viewed and processed in that application by employees. Subsequently, the results are transferred back to the SAP application.	For example, planning results are entered or correction postings based on consolidation are booked	No

As a principle, we apply licenses to employee based on the authorization profiles and usage analysis with metrics as mentioned in the table below Table 1-1 License table:

Category	Metric	Comments
Professional	Named users #	
Limited Professional	Named users #	
Employee	Named users #	
Operational	Named users #	
Indirect	Named Indirect users #	

License Dashboard

License Dashboard

As illustrated above in the dashboard, the final objective is to present value of $$ of non-compliance by specific products. This would help you in regaining compliance status either by reclaiming additional licenses or optimization. You should be able to slice and dice by product family, product, license category and the metric to measure the licenses. For example, SAP has various categories of licenses by products, which can be monitored on a real-time basis to assess non-compliance.

It is important to build a license dashboard as illustrated below to communicate current license position across departments. This would help assess risks of non-compliance and take necessary corrective actions on-time. Otherwise, you would never realize status of non-compliance till the final audit with respective publishers. You must ensure purchase contract code is capture with acquired licenses, swapped licenses for traceability.

Case study #1: A large manufacturing company based in Europe.

The company wanted to build a robust licenses management practices to ensure compliance. The key compliance officer was responsible for periodic internal audit with control measures to ensure absolute compliance. The company had almost 9-10 ERP instances of various release versions such as R/3 4.6C, ECC 6.0 and ECC 6.0 EHP 8.0. Also, interfaces such as external supplier portals that are used to update supplier details in the SAP using the B2C third-party portal.

Well, there were several challenges. I believe one of the major challenges were related to interconnecting departments that were operating in SILOS, there were different views between the business, I.T Project, Support, I.T vendor and the sourcing teams. In the end, there was no accountability. A good license management practice will need strong leadership to pull all strings together. It's a humongous effort to bring everyone on to the same platform and mindset. In the end, we realized there was no accountability. This was the primary reasons for non-compliance. Unless there is rigor and commitment from the leadership, the system is bound to become non-compliant. First task for the team was given by the top management to build a baseline view of the current licenses position. Therefore, the team developed a simple dashboard with the current licenses position. A quick and dirty way to solve these problems is to use tools such as QlikView, Qlik sense or any analytical tool that can help you assess the current situation. It took almost 3-4 months of efforts to consolidate inputs from more than 20+ productive systems interacting with SAP. A very high-level view of the ERP usage in the organization is illustrated in ERP Landscape below.

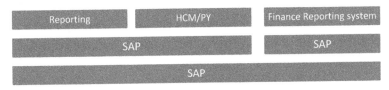

ERP Landscape

In the above ERP Landscape there were close to ten thousand NAMED users accessing SAP DIRECTLY with an additional 10K users accessing data as SAP INDIRECT users via batch process using B2C channels. For example, portal users access data in ERP using B2C portal such as sourcing teams. Eventually, these PO's were raised in the core SAP system. Hence, it is essential to build robust governance and best practices to match the correct profile into respective licenses category. This was a huge challenge for us to identify the profiles matching with the respective license category. For example, Procurement, Finance, teams will need appropriate access to SAP. You'll have opportunity to segregate users based on the authorization profile or real-time transaction usage. In either of these two approaches, you'll need to find what a sourcing guy does. For example. Sourcing guy will do day-to-day tasks such as creation a purchase request, purchase order etc.

These are specific transactions such as **ME21N** available in SAP for PR/PO create, display. Hence, each of these users will need appropriate access to manage their day-to-day activities. However, the challenge in most of the organization is to identify the profiles and map it to respective transaction is bit complex. Therefore, most of these users over a period is assigned the highest category of licenses. To address different categories of available licenses for your organization, please refer to your contract details. In the above customer situation, we found the following categories were available:

    a.   SAP Application Professional
    b.   SAP Application Limited Professional
    c.   SAP Employee User
    d.   SAP Business User
    e.   SAP Developer &
    f.   SAP Operator

In the Named Direct category, these are the predominant licenses types. You may have procured business user, which is little more expense than the above categories and not very often used. Each of these categories of licenses pricing would vary based on your organization's negotiations done with SAP in the respective region. Mostly organizations assign the highest category to employees and scramble through profiles ahead of the audit, which is not a great idea. This should be strictly avoided. One of the major pitfalls in license management is lack of managing accurate inventory, thus leading to non-compliance over a period.

- **# 1 - Lack of managing Inventory**

It is important to build a simple excel or a tool to industrialize inputs to the repository. You should have details up-to-date about the contract, current inventory and the result of compliance in $$ value. This would make more sense to present to your Licenses steering committee. Otherwise, there would be no visibility of the project team. First security team is responsible

- **# 2 Lack of robust governance**

Indeed, this could be risky as the lack of governance may lead to severe non-compliance. If you do not dedicate resources to manage licenses, then the audit will become very complex task with several team's running in the end with no productive efforts. It is important to ensure a dedicated licenses practice to manage the right team to coordinate across various departments. A sample governance model is laid out for your quick reference:

Optimization was done by leveraging a monthly ST03 analysis to identify the right usage and the user re-classification to downgrade the license from higher to the lower category. Another area of optimization was user active status checks to ensure these users are active for at least 60 days to consider for license entitlements. These two topics involving user active status check with activity type assessment would help you to optimize license usage. Based on 3 quarter performance analysis, client was able to optimize up to 25% to save license costs and this became a valid point in the negotiation of contract for additional license procurement. Further, based on analyzing the indirect usage by analyzing the output document types, client was able to optimize usage up to 30% by analyzing the accurate documents that are posted in SAP. The team did a thorough analysis by checking the documents created, updated by the third-party applications connected to ERP to ensure right 'ENGINE' license category such as 'Sales Order', 'Purchase Order' and Payroll engines monitored. The metric for ENGINE measurement is the total orders (create) operations performed in core ERP by a third-party application. This was possible by utilizing simple scripts to track the documents created in a productive ERP environment.

Client had initially procured over 10,000 SAP Professional license type. However, most of the users were wrongly assigned with the type, hence they analyzed usage for over six months and reclassified these users with a lower entitlement such as employee and limited professional that ended up in 25% savings during the negotiation phase. The license GAP is basically the non-compliance if it is in negative exceeding the acquired licenses. In this case, a risk alert should be flagged for respective departments. Finally, software asset manager would consolidate requirements and request sourcing to request for additional licenses.

Extracted data from various soruces including ERP, non-ERP and Engine orders information to analyze compliance position.

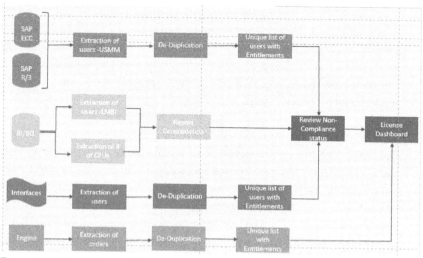

Figure 1-1 Extract Methodology

The above figure represents real-time extraction based on the case study, where the client extracted from the disparate SAP systems such as SAP ECC 6.0 EHP 8.0, SAP R/3 4.7, SAP R/3 4.6C and SAP BI 7.0 with several interface applications supporting their manufacturing business. Once the users were extracted, team analyzed the usage and de-activated few non-active users. Further by executing workload monitor analysis in SAP using /ST03 t-code, it is possible to realize the real usage of transactions and the frequency of usage to map it to the respective pattern of usage. This pattern usage with group of transactions determine the right entitlement such as Professional, Limited Professional or Employee. The re-classification would help you save 25%-30% of users downgraded from higher grade of professional entitlement to limited professional or employee. Thus, it gives your sourcing team flexibility of exchanging professional quantity to additional quantity of limited professional or employee.

There are three categories of licenses:
1. Direct (USMM)
2. Indirect * document types
3. Engine * product order usage
4. BI/BO (LMBI)

Each of the category is factored and compliance is measured differently.

For example, Named Direct usage is monitored by identifying active users in the system. We extract usage data by executing USMM transactions in SAP environments to identify exact list of active users with licenses mapped.

106

Unfortunately, our client has mapped everyone into Professional licenses category, which means we pay more for even limited users. However, the challenge is how do we measure the profiles of the users, unless you have followed best practices in mapping profiles to the users. This is a risk now in our landscape for two reasons:

a. Non-compliance – due to incorrect licenses mapped and pay more for utilization
b. Budget – increased budget due to invalid assignments.

The above two risks can be mitigated by the following actions:

a. Identify usage based on ST03 transaction analysis in SAP
b. Map the profiles using the 3 months usage analysis.
c. Form a pattern of usage and use it for assignments. For example, we know what transactions are run by a PO user, so on and so forth.
d. Re-run USMM to extract list of users with correct entitlements (licenses category)

The above steps would help us mitigate the risks in our environment. Therefore, it is prudent to run the following steps to ensure compliance.

a. Execute monthly run to extract usage and compliance position
b. Remediation on a quarterly basis to ensure ST03 analysis is done and users mapped with correct licenses entitlements.

Now, Governance part. How do we achieve our goals without breaking our head!

SAP License Management – Governance (Reclassification)

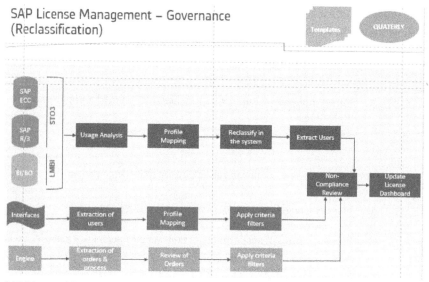

SAP License Management Governance (Reclassification)

In the above flow, focus your attention on the remediation activities. Once Technical team extracts data from the ERP systems, the plan is to map respective profiles and re-classify them based on the transactional usage to review non-compliance on a quarterly basis. If your license position is non-compliant, then the respective application owner will be responsible to work closely with asset manager to ensure compliance by optimization of users or request sourcing lead for additional procurement of licenses based on real-time usage. We have observed a lot of inactive users, and users with higher category of licenses assigned. These are potential opportunities to re-classify in to the lower category of licenses to enable substantial cost savings.

The above sequence of tasks represents monthly, quarterly process flow of license management where respective teams perform their tasks to ensure compliance.

Phase II License Contract Review Phase

    a.   Contract Review
    b.   License Guidance &
    c.   Negotiation Support

Contract Review: It is important to study the contract in detail to understand your entitlement. ERP publishers are very specific in license terms and conditions mentioned in the contract and it may vary based on your specific license entitlements. For example. Professional licenses category may have a set of entitlement as per your software user rights contract agreed with the respective software publisher. Your ERP system may be generic or Industry specific, hence the entitlement may vary.

License Guidance: Secondly, you'll need to check the system usage by using in-house tools. In our case study, we have observed client was using /ST03 (standard transaction code in SAP). You can review software user rights and prepare a guidance for internal entitlement alignment. From a negotiation stand-point there are multiple ways to deal with ERP publishers.

Negotiation: You have an option to exchange licenses for a lower category. For example, in the above case study, client used over 10,000 user's entitlement in SAP Application professional category, later based on detailed analysis, they re-classified these users to a lower category in to Employee and Limited professional category. This was possible by creating a pattern of usage and further analyzing in the QlikView business intelligence tool.

You can build a simple macro to analyzing the usage pattern of your key users. Based on the usage and process mapped, you would be able to reclassify. This approach would help you negotiate strongly with SAP to procure additional licenses by exchanging unused licenses. Based on our survey, we have identified a robust license governance is required to succeed in the license program. It is not an individual task as software asset manager along with the IT departments are responsible for the entire program.

You may launch this program as a six-sigma project as illustrated below with a tool based automated approach for dashboard preparations and maintenance to assess license current position:

User Assignment based on the profile

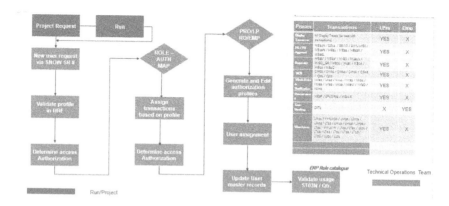

User assignment

The above flow chart illustrates new user request by the respective project or support team depending on the phase of the project. Once the project is deployed, run team will take over and there may be additional requirements for adding new users or changing the profile of the users which may impact the overall license entitlements. As illustrated, once a required arrives via Service Now tool (SNOW) or whichever tool that you may use for service requests, a ticket is created and sent to the respective security team for validation using User request form (URF) with detailed tasks performed by the user. For example, a manager may request for a sourcing user to support procurement tasks. He may specify relevant information in the URF form and request via SNOW ticket. Once the ticket arrives into security team's desk, they would provision users as per the profile by validating the activity list and assign the correct role. For example, a Sourcing team member will need transaction access to create, update purchase orders (ME01) access. Thus, security team will assign the right role using the ERP Role catalogue which provides the mapping details as mentioned in the reference table with list of transactions with license entitlements.

User Assignment based on real-time usage

PROCESS	ACTIVITIES
TRANSVERSE	**Display T-code**
PR/PO APPROVAL	**ME54N, ME29N, ME54, ME55, ME35K, ME35L**
REQUESTOR	**ME51, ME52, MIGO, ML81N, MB01, ML81, MB1A, MB02, MB1C**
NCR	**QM01, QM02, QM12, QM10, IQ12, IQ01, IQ02**
TIME BOOKING	**CATS**
WAREHOUSE	**LM01, LM03, LM00, LM05, LT***
WORK ORDER	**IW32, IW52, IW41, IW51, IW31, IW68**

As illustrated above, in the case study, we observed 2000 users using <= 10 transactions, hence these users need an SAP Limited Professional entitlement. Similarly, sourcing (PR/PO) users are around 500+ those who run purchase order / purchase requisition as their day-to-day routine tasks. The usage may be split into Time Booking users, Warehouse users, procurement, Quality (NCR) and a quiet few of users are transversal. Therefore, the entitlement for these users can be finalized based on the real-time data using the above matrix. Each client will need to build a pattern of transactions with its usage. After you carefully study the usage, you can re-classify usage as per the real-time transactional data. These patterns can be constructed by carefully reviewing your entitlements with software user rights.

The respective teams as stated above will be responsible for tasks

Dashboard

License Usage dashboard

The above dashboard illustrates usage and license type assignments in SAP. For example, you will identify count of inactive users, optimal users and light users based on the transactions executed by the users. As you know, within ERP you have different category. Metric refers to the exact measurement of licenses such as 'users' and the swapped column indicates the numbers of licenses swapped with the publisher during the negotiation phase. The key objective is to keep this dashboard up-to-date to identify the GAP, which is the non-compliance and procure additional licenses or take necessary actions to optimize, to keep a control mechanism to mitigate risks of non-compliance. The metric column varies by the product, as it may depend on the Engine or ERP Named. For example, a named license type is measured by the total number of users deployed. However, for measuring engine access, it is based on the total transactions consumed by respective end-to-end process. For example, P2P, O2C processes are measured by total orders created per year...say 10,000-20,000 total transaction volume per year. This will mitigate the risks of non-compliance due to indirect usage. Some products such as SAP BI/BO and PI are measured based on Named usage + CPU measurements.

In our case study, client updated the dashboard monthly with the quarterly optimization applied to keep reduce non-compliance. The respective core ERP and interface teams highlighted the usage in respective columns and the software asset management consolidated the final GAP. This GAP analysis report was used by sourcing, finance teams to determine final negotiation position with the publisher.

License Measurement Project Plan

G2	G3				G4				G5				G6											
Sep 2018		Oct 2018			NOV 2018			DEC 2018				JAN 2019			FEB 2019			MAR 2019					
49	50	51	52	1	2	3	4	5	6	7	8	9	10	11	12	13	14	15	16	17	18	19	20	21	22	23	24	25	26

DEFINE — MEASURE — ANALYZE / IMPROVE — CONTROL

SAP License Monitor & Control
Go Live - DEC 2018
SAP LM Audit support

License Control Board - SOLUTION FREEZE

Requirements | Classification

Trial POC
INSTALL
Direct analysis
Indirect analysis
Report prep
Report finalization
TEST | User classify | CONTROL | SAP LM Audit support

SAP LM User re-classification
Cyc(i) user redass | Cyc(ii)

SAP LM Usage Policy
SAP LM Policy | SAM Trng | LM support

High Level planning

Table 1-1: Critical Phases with Activities:

The project plan illustrates critical phases of license program launch prior to the audit to enable users actively participate across various domains including interface systems to your core SAP ERP to gather information about the usage by leveraging tools in the respective system. This is a sample project plan to identify license usage using six sigma methodologies to measure usage accurately and optimize. The outcome of this plan is to enable current license position and negotiation strategy with ERP editor to gain the best value for money.

Critical Phases	Activities	Start Date	Finish Date
Define	RFP Launch	24-Aug	31-Aug
	Response from the Suppliers	31-Aug	5-Sep
	Commercial/Technical Discussions and selection	5-Sep	10-Sep
	Legal policy responses	10-Sep	12-Sep
	Finalization of the contract	12-Sep	17-Oct
Measure	Conduct kick-off meeting	17-Sep	24-Sep
	SAP LM Tool - Prepare workshop schedule for POC Pilot	24-Sep	28-Sep
	Conduct SAP LM Tool Trial POC in test (MC3) for baseline analysis report	10-Oct	15-Oct
	Analyze Indirect usage	10-Oct	15-Oct
	Finalize Scope, Gaps and Open points	15-Oct	17-Oct
Analyze	Configuration of the tool in PRD Environment	19-Oct	20-Oct
	Proposed recommendations & commit reclassification changes in PRD	28-Oct	31-Oct
Improve	Cycle (I) optimization	31-Oct	9-Nov
	Analyze Indirect usage with document types	11-Nov	15-Nov
Control	Cycle (II) Optimization	15-Nov	19-Nov
	Finalize current licenses standing position	19-Nov	21-Nov
	Explain roles to the business and control usage / RU	21-Nov	22-Nov

Summary

In this chapter, you've studied the importance Of ERP license compliance and audit access pitfalls and the best practices. This would help you manage the compliance and audit requirements. Now, let's look at the holistic approach on accomplishing the ambitious digital licenses topic with case studies in the next chapter.

■   ■   ■

Chapter 5: SAM Maturity Model

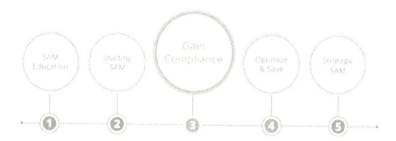

One of the key questions that every Organization should raise is the current maturity level of software asset management practices. You would never be able to achieve asset management goals Unless you've achieved the desired levels SAM Maturity. Now, let us explore the approach to assess current SAM maturity levels with the target planning to reach the desired SAM maturity levels. There are six stages in the transformation journey to reach SAM Maturity Level 5 from the baseline with the core objectives of compliance with audit readiness. If you're able to achieve highest level of SAM maturity, which means your Organization can develop consistent license position and traceability of asset management lifecycle without much manual intervention with the ability to forecast.

One of the main aspects of IT Asset Management, also known as ITAM is Software Asset Management (SAM), has seen a large increase in demand and interest in its services in recent years, and SAM professionals are now considered a niche, with established, specialist professionals in high demand from a variety of organizations across several different sectors. Hence, it is imperative to measure your current SAM maturity level. A SAM Maturity assessment provides an organization a simple point in time view of your software asset management (SAM) maturity level. This gives you an independent review and benchmark from which you can progress on your SAM journey as illustrated below:

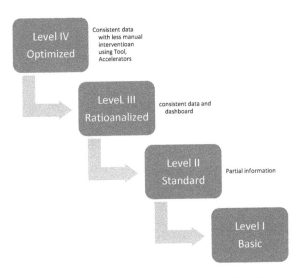

Level IV Optimized — Consistent data with less manual interventioan using Tool, Accelerators

LeveL III Ratioanalized — consistent data and dashboard

Level II Standard — Partial information

Level I Basic

1. Basic – Lack of policies, procedures, resources and tools

2. Standardized – Partial information which is not complete and accurate

3. Rationalized – reliable information is used to manage assets to business targets

4. Optimized – SAM is a strategic asset to overall business objectives with tools, accelerators

There are several ways in which SAM can help an organization, but it takes a lot of time, effort and support from senior management. So, what exactly is SAM? And how can we tie this back to senior management values to generate the required support?

SAM Core Phases

SAM Maturity Assessment

The above picture illustrates respective phases with activities in each of the SAM assessment. In the first step, organizations will need to assess the current state of licenses using manual methods. In the next phase, one of the critical tasks is to develop an effective license position. This would help in assessing return on investments (ROI) and finally build a robust SAM strategy and roadmap to ensure consistent audit practices and monitoring to avoid non-compliance.

Following SAM maturity assessment table illustrates steps with detail activities listed below:

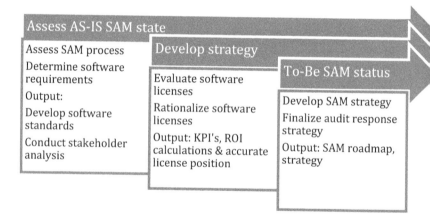

SAM TO-BE Maturity Strategy

The core objectives of SAM maturity assessment are to identify the baseline standard and improve the SAM maturity level from level x to level 4, which is the highest level of optimization to stabilize asset management practices. However, most of the organizations start smaller in terms of maturity level assessment to achieve level 3 to be able to develop consistent reporting with reliable data. This is the most important part of SAM maturity level to achieve minimum Level 4 to be consistent in the asset management dashboard capabilities.

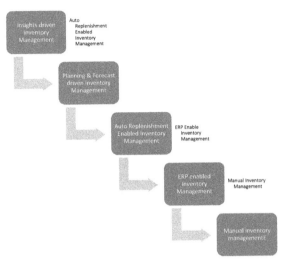

TO-BE SAM Maturity Stages

As illustrated above, organizations should strive for achieving the highest level of SAM maturity level with insights driven inventory management, instead of being a reactive approach with several manual data points across various departments.

Five Stages of Maturity:

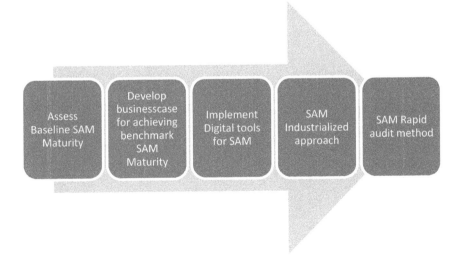

1. Stage 1 – Assess Baseline SAM Maturity
2. Stage 2 – Develop Business case for achieving Benchmark SAM maturity
3. Stage 3 – Implement Digital tools, methods & accelerators for SAM
4. Stage 4 – SAM Industrialization approach &
5. Stage 5 – SAM Rapid Audit Method (RAM)

Stage 1 – Assess SAM Baseline Maturity

The basic requirement s to understand where you're right now in terms of software asset management. With so many software titles and devices in use across the organization, constant change and vast quantities of data - where should you start? As with most IT management disciplines - many organizations choose to benchmark their SAM maturity before starting their journey to help formulate their SAM strategy. This allows a Software Asset Manager to assess their current position, identify weak spots and determine their key priorities. The ISO standard is a great independent resource and many organizations use it as a reference model for SAM.

However, based on the average SAM maturity of organizations today, the ISO standard may be an overly comprehensive guideline to benchmark against. The Microsoft SOM, which is also based on the ISO Standard, in contrast is a more straightforward assessment provides a very quick and accessible valuation of what is required to get started. It is based on ten key competencies, which provide straightforward pointers on how to progress the business towards maturity and improvement of Software Asset Management.

Stage 2 - Developing a Powerful Business Case for achieving SAM benchmark with the following objectives:

      d.   Compliance & license position (Implement policies, procedure, internal audit etc.)

      e.   Agile (Digital dashboard with ability to aligning all key stakeholders)

      f.   Efficiency (audit ready with stronger negotiation position with editors)

Though, non-compliance and license current position is key, there is several outcomes expected from SAM. For example, consider a major business transformation projects on the horizon and strategic software publishers the company utilizes will help build a solid business case that the organization can support.

SAM is proactive housekeeping, monitoring and control of software. For any company spending money on software and maintenance every year. These three elements should form the backbone of your SAM business plan.

1. **Compliance:** This is the most basic principle of good governance. An organisation needs to ensure its meeting its contractual and legal obligations for the software it is buying. The impact of SAM on software compliance can be measured in terms of audit penalties and fines avoided. Organisations with a solid SAM practice in place can avoid software audit penalties from publisher. The distraction of audits should also not be underestimated. Without the appropriate processes and tools in place, key IT resources must be pulled away from the delivery of IT projects to address audit requirements.

2. **Efficiency:** An organization with improved management controls in place has good visibility of what assets the company owns, what is in use and how it is configured. After meeting the initial goal of compliance SAM will inevitably lead to more efficient IT spend.

   SAM empowers smarter decision making such as:
   i. Removing unused software - reducing maintenance spend.
   ii. Fulfilling new software requests from unused stockpiles - avoiding spend.

iii. Changing architecture, configurations or versions to save money whilst still meeting business requirements - optimisation of existing assets.

iv. Constructing more favourable deals with software publishers based on accurate usage.

v. Taking the lead in contract negotiations based on trustworthy intelligence of usage and future requirements.

3. **Agility**: The final major category of SAM business value is agility. The agility delivered by SAM has immense impact but is probably the most difficult to quantify. However, it should be factored into your SAM business plan - especially if you wish to win over the hearts and minds of your broader business stakeholders in the longer term and maintain the momentum of your SAM practice once compliance and efficiency savings have been delivered and realised.

How does SAM deliver agility?

To be agile, you must leverage tools, methods to support your SAM initiatives. For example, in a complex I.T landscape, you may need a dashboard tool with additional editor specific license management tools to measure usage metrics and combine with the central dashboard. Therefore, SAM delivers great business intelligence to support the decision making of the whole IT department as well as the business in general, which can be used in any transformational project. Your core objectives should be keeping accurate and up-to-date inventory, current license position. It helps organizations with quick decision making including better contract negotiation possibilities.

Your organization might own software contracts with different software publishers - but to make real progress with SAM you must take advantage of the 80:20 rule or the Pareto principle. 80% of the risk, costs, audit threat and likely SAM headaches are likely to be found in less than 20% of your software publishers.

Focus your efforts on 5 or 10 high value or high-risk software publishers and you will deliver substantial leverage compared to trying to manage everything. You can always broaden your scope once momentum begins to build and savings accrue. Working with an experienced SAM practitioner or partner can help you identify what should be in your target vendor list, the low hanging fruit in terms of savings for your business plan, and where opportunities exist for optimisation. Combine the priorities identified in a maturity assessment with a well-considered target list of software publishers - and you'll have a good focus for delivering reduced comp

Stage 3 – Implementing Digital Tools for SAM

As discussed in the earlier chapters a good record of Inventory, License consumption with real-time data is important to achieve higher level of SAM Level (4) maturity. A manual method is always time consuming and hold-up your internal resources with a lot of time spent on reconciliation. Hence, you will need a digital SAM tool to consolidate data real-time to report consumption and alert non-compliance such as over consumption of user licenses by respective products.

SAM practice is a combination of Process, People and Technology. People: You can't do SAM alone, you need to win over the hearts and minds of end user customers or consumers or software, the IT department as well as the key stakeholders or cost centers making decisions about software. Process: SAM is not a one-off exercise, it's an ongoing discipline. To maintain balance and visibility of assets organizations to put management processes in place: the checks and balances to ensure things are getting done, changes are being recorded, objectives are being met and users are getting what was promised.

Technology: SAM technology and services are an important element of delivering a valuable SAM practice. SAM technology should help you with some of the heavy lifting associated with maintaining good records: register of assets, users, devices and systems, automating processes where possible and helping Software Asset Managers identify and interpret their assets and entitlements. There are three key areas to consider when choosing a SAM technology. Some of these might be addressed with your existing in-house systems, some may consider investment as part of your SAM business plan.

1. Inventory Management -
Auditing and maintaining an inventory of hardware and software in your IT estate. Sometimes using an agent, sometimes without or a combination of both. Will you use existing tools for systems management technology such as Microsoft System Center Configuration Manager, Symantec Altiris or LANDESK or will you use a dedicated inventory tool specifically for SAM? This will be determined by the software publishers in scope.

2. The main SAM tool or license management tool: taking the feed of inventory of your assets, recording your entitlement, helping you to interpret and ultimately reconcile them.

3. **Network Discovery**: Proving that your inventory is exhaustive. During a software audit an auditor will run scripts to prove they have exhaustive visibility of the software and hardware assets on your network.

You should do internal audits to improve the credibility and reliability of your data. Some additional tool considerations may include the following. Again, these may overlap with your existing systems: Asset Register: A detailed record of all IT Assets (above and beyond software this may also include hardware, telephony, networking equipment, or anything else of value to the business).

1. Where are we today? What are we looking to achieve? What are the gaps in achieving our goals and priorities around SAM?
2. What editors are we focused on, based on spend and risk profile?
3. For the editors identified in step 2 - what does compliance look like? Do we know how to measure consumption and manage the software publishers?
4. What data will we need to collect on an ongoing basis to satisfy our management objectives in step 3?
5. What mechanisms do we need to maintain the data identified in step 4 on an ongoing basis?
6. How will we verify that our data is accurate?

We need SAM tools to help us with record keeping, automation and helping to build great business intelligence with the IT assets we own. However, Software Asset Managers should only assess the need for a SAM toolset once the first two steps in this guide have been completed - an assessment of current maturity and a short list of target software publishers with a brief risk assessment. SAM tool requirements should be driven from the outcome of these two exercises.

Stage 4 – SAM Rapid Audit Method (RAM)

As part of Level (4) maturity levels, we discussed achieving level (4) maturity level which is the highest level of automation through smart process to keep inventory and licenses current position.

Implementing processes always allows an organization to mature from the state of running periodic 'internal audit' to maintaining an up to date record. A Software Asset Manager can harness the weaknesses identified in the maturity assessment to determine what processes are required to maintain a good view of assets and make progress with SAM.

For example, it is said that most of the cost and risk of owning software is found in datacenter-oriented software. It could also be said that most modern IT organizations have some degree of change management process in place for changes in datacenter environments.

So, it follows that implementing a simple process to review planned changes to see if any have software licensing implications will prevent a lot of headaches down the line and allow us to maintain an accurate view of our compliance and efficiency goals in the datacenter. Software Asset Managers also need to understand that SAM doesn't happen overnight. It is a gradual process of changing the habits and entrenched behavior an organization uses and procures software. So, we recommend taking a Continual Service Improvement approach - review what is happening on a regular basis and make improvements based on priority. Every IT department is in a constant state of transition. People are joining and leaving the company, new systems are being built, users are being supported, and new applications are being deployed. Processes allow us to stay on top of the changes occurring and be proactive. Otherwise Software Asset Managers will always be firefighting against a constant barrage of changes across their estate. A key sign of SAM maturity is to progress from counting licenses and clearing up the clutter after the compelling event, to working with the business to proactively assist in making decisions as they are needed.

Stage 5 – Audit Readiness

As mentioned in earlier sections, software audits are a fact of life and present a massive distraction from key projects and business as usual. However, it may always not be worthwhile or realistic to monitor compliance. This is equivalent to providing 100% availability of a service that's only seldom required – it is overkill. Instead, we recommend that organizations strive to aim for the status of 'audit ready'. That is, if a Software Asset Manager receives a request for an audit - whether via internal audit or external software publisher request - the SAM team is prepared for it. Key characteristics of being audit ready:
- Cycle Time to responding to auditors as per benchmark standards
- Organized response to auditors by the SAM team without panic
- Up-to-date Inventory management and current licenses position

This proactive approach removes the panic and headache of audit requests, allowing the SAM team to provide very accurate supporting data for contract negotiations and exploring new projects or strategic changes. An organization with a status of 'audit ready' for key software publishers is also likely to face fewer audit requests, because they can demonstrate full control and visibility and the intention to manage compliance.

Stage 6 - Global SAM Team

A final consideration when building a world class modern SAM practice is a balanced team. A fundamental part of your business case is building resource in your team to deliver against the plan and meet your objectives. It is useful to revisit your prioritized list of software publishers when assessing the skillset required within the team. Can your team deliver against each of the competencies below or are there any gaps that need addressing?

• Manage inventory
• License reconciliation

Build a skills matrix of your internal resources and check off which areas you have covered. Gaps in your competencies could be addressed by internal specialists in the IT team, further training for your SAM team, or working with partners. For more complex software license programs, where it may not be commercially viable to have the skills in house, the gap can be addressed through use of SAM partners for periodic checks and reconciliation.

Level IV Maturity model:

1. Level I – Identify software and hardware installed
2. Level II – Perform purchased vs. Installed license reconciliation on an ad hoc basis
3. Level III – Automated Entitled vs. consumed license reconciliation. SAM processes to manage contracts and maintain continuous license compliance
4. Level IV – Automated entitlement-based license management & optimization

SAM Maturity Model

Application Readiness Maturity Model

At Level 4, IT organizations are ready for change and can quickly adopt new technologies like Virtual Desktop Infrastructure (VDI) or Mobile Application Management and keep up with the increasing frequency of software infrastructure updates and releases. Here IT has implemented a complete, end-to-end automated process for managing applications across their entire lifecycles in the enterprise, from purchase to retirement. IT has codified packaging standards and best practices, automated the request/fulfilment processes, and established a single point of service for applications and licenses.

At this level, IT has integrated the Application Readiness process with other related business processes. This includes integration with Software License Optimization and IT service management processes to ensure that licenses are available for requested applications, optimize license spend, and improve service delivery and support. In addition, IT has empowered end users to serve themselves in requesting applications using a consumer-like process. Users simply select the desired application from an enterprise app store. The requests are automatically validated, checked for license availability, routed for approval (if necessary), and the applications are delivered to the requesters quickly and reliably.

Process:

At Level 4 of the Application Readiness Maturity Model, the end-to-end process of managing the enterprise application lifecycle is fully automated.

- The line of business or application owner enters a request using a specialized, request process that automates the collection of requirements and initiates the Application Readiness process.
- The request is validated through automatic lookup of application information in an external application data source such as service now (SNOW) tools to confirm that the application is approved and purchased.
- The requested application is automatically assessed for compatibility across multiple target environments and multiple virtualization formats to determine best fit. Mobile apps are tested for both device and OS compatibility, as well as assessed for risky behavior.

- Planning phase only needs to deal with exceptions because packaging standards and best practices are codified enabling automation of many of the packaging tasks.
- If there are no exceptions, the application is automatically packaged and handed off to the deployment system for automatic promotion to the test and production environments. Simultaneously, the application is published to the enterprise app store for immediate access by end users.
- Feedback on deployment success/failure is used to proactively and continually improve service quality.

Expected Outcome:

The benefits of reaching Level 4 of Application Readiness are many. IT dramatically shrinks the time from request for a new application to delivery and reduces costs through increased efficiency and informed demand planning. IT also aligns more closely with the business in that IT no longer must wait for the business to tell IT what it needs. Instead, IT can proactively make application recommendations to line of business owners on applications that may be right for them. In addition, IT can now effectively manage SLAs and accurately predict the time to roll out new applications.

What's more, IT increases end-user productivity and satisfaction by empowering users with self-service access to applications. And that's not all. IT future proofs the application portfolio in that it can quickly add new applications and take on new technologies such as mobile devices, enabling the enterprise to maintain a competitive edge.

Summary

As discussed in this chapter, SAM plays a major role in asset compliance and license requirements. Hence, it is important to achieve higher maturity levels with automation possible to avoid time consuming extraction for compiling a license dashboard. Often, auditors request you to showcase details of usage across applications in terms of core ERP, support functions and engineering applications. The core objectives should be up-to-date inventory, consumption details with evidences gathered over a period to showcase auditors. However, SAM is not limited to compliance and licenses consumption, it is a fundamental practice of purchasing, contracts, licensing, compliance and audit. Once you achieve Level (4) maturity levels, you will be able to forecast accurate aligned with organizational goals.

It has now got to the stage where software asset management needs to be considered as a core competency for any organization. With the increase in software license audits, now is the time to ensure that your estate has the processes in place to maintain compliancy and be audit ready.

Chapter 6: License in Digital Era

One of the main aspects of an effective Digital business is how software assets are managed as the landscape becomes increasingly complex. Hence, there is a need for an organization to achieve level (4) SAM maturity as a desired level to procure, consume, monitor and retire software assets. More so to ensure compliance with best practices to monitor, optimize over a period to save costs in assets. An effective asset management will increase productivity by keeping up-to-date inventory with software asset upgrade requirements. A good SAM practice would help an organization to drive strategic decisions such as roadmap decisions and to support the business functions more effectively.

Lifecycle Overview

The above figure illustrates detailed view of ITAM Lifecycle with all processes integrated.

ITIL 'Software Asset Management (SAM) is all of the infrastructure and processes necessary for the effective management, control, and protection of the software assets within an organization throughout all stages of their lifecycle' 'Software Asset Management (SAM) is a best practice incorporating a set of proven processes and procedures for managing and optimizing your organization's IT assets. Implementing SAM protects your software investments and helps you recognize what you have, where it's running, and if your organization is using your assets efficiently'

SAM is the practice of integrating people, processes, and technology to allow software licenses and usage to be systematically tracked, evaluated and managed. The goal of Software Asset Management is to reduce IT expenditures, human resource overhead, and compliance risks that are inherent in owning and managing software assets'

SAM Charter 'Software Asset Management is the right blend of people, systems and processes required to effectively manage your software and software related assets throughout their lifecycle to an agreed scope'

What would 'day-to-day SAM' look like?

In our case study, initially SAM organization was new and then gradually build the capabilities from Level (2) TO Level (4) with tools, accelerators to prepare a detailed dashboard for the steering committee review and take necessary decisions. Finally, the client SAM team was able to bring the compliance levels from RED to GREEN by effectively managing the licenses with usage optimization. The day-to-day responsibilities of SAM vary dependent on the organization. However, the basic daily functions of SAM are to ensure compliance and risk mitigation the management of the processes and policies around software and its use needs to be enforced daily by the SAM team, as does the communication and education aspect of SAM. They need to ensure that end users are kept up-to-date with what current projects the SAM team are involved in, and any changes that may be occurring to the license metrics of the software end users have installed.

As stated in our case study, client was able to report usage from various applications into consolidated repository using QlikView, which was further used to slice, and dice information based on application, user type and entitlements. This dashboard was used as a centralized repository by the SAM Manager to realize current licenses status with non-compliance position and highlight risks.

This is the hub for everything software and license related, so it needs users who have expert knowledge of the tool to ensure the organization gets the most out of it. Another change to the core processes was to streamline change management such as software upgrade, new software procurements, uplift to the users.

Being a point of contact for queries is another big aspect of a SAM team's daily job. Queries can range from 'do we have any licenses' to 'where is the boxed copy of Software A kept?'. It is up to the SAM team to ensure that they are known as being the point of contact for anything related to software or software licensing.

Responsibilities

As mentioned in the definitions stage, the overall responsibilities of software asset management are to ensure the correct management of software assets (including software licenses) throughout their lifecycle. SAM is responsible for software from the minute it is requested, through procurement, deployment, recycling and finally retirement. Along with the software itself, SAM is also responsible for the license that comes with it, ensuring all users are using the software within the product use rights and ensuring that the organization maintains compliancy.

Furthermore, SAM is also responsible for the continual updating of any software related processes, procedures and policies. The three P's need to be updated on a regular basis to ensure that a company's license position remains relevant and to keep up with changes in licensing terms, or even changes in technology. It is up to the SAM personnel in conjunction with senior management's approval to review, evaluate and then change any or all the processes, procedures or software policies.

SAM personnel

There are several positions within the SAM discipline, and a mature organization may have a variety of SAM positions within their organization.

Job Title	Responsibilities
SAM ADMIN	• Adding software assets into a database or SAM tool • First point of contact for software asset requests • Daily management of SAM tool • Management of any physical licenses • Management of any physical software boxes • Producing Standard SAM reports
SAM Analyst	• Analyses license usage Analyses software assets deployed throughout the organization • Conducts internal reviews (audits) on selected software vendors to ensure they are 'audit ready' • Researches new license types and trends that may impact the organization➤ Analyses multiple data sets
SAM Manager	• Manages the SAM team Monitors compliancy Overall responsibility of the management of SAM tool Dependent on structure, can deal with license agreements or this is left to senior staff members Dictates which vendors should be

	reviewed internally
	• Point of contact for any SAM or licensing related questions
SAM Consultant	• May be employed in place of a SAM Manager • Can either be placed in the SAM team, or as the link between senior management at the SAM team • Usually a SAM or Tier 1 software licensing expert • Vast experience in software asset management
SAM Specialist	• Expert in SAM • Can be a specialist in certain SAM or software licensing areas • Role tailored based on organizations needs and requirements
SAM Director	• Board representative • Provides overall strategy and goals for the SAM team • Point of contact for any further issues • Along with SAM Manager, dictates what SAM education and communication they will provide end users • Deals with license agreements • Oversees alignment of SAM to business and IT requirements

SAM Standards

There are three ISO SAM standards that an organization needs to be aware of. They are:

ISO 19770-1 ISO 19770-2 ISO 19770-3**ISO 19770-1** is a framework of processes relating to the organization performing software asset management to an adequate standard. This standard provides organizations with a tool to clearly display and present the fact that they are managing their software assets in accordance with governance standards.

ISO 19770-2 is all about the software identification tags. Identification tags help establish what instances of software are installed. Software identification tags, also known as software ID tags (SWID) provide identifying information not only for installed software, but also for another form of licensable application. Software vendors use ISO 19770-2 to enable their software to be easily, quickly and accurately identified.

ISO 19770-3 relates to software entitlement tagging. Software entitlement tags are files that help identify the applications software licensing rights. As with ISO 19770-2 this helps with the day-to-day management of a SAM project as it helps SAM tools automatically identify the license metrics for certain applications that have entitlement tags built into them.

Its important to select the best tool that supports your ITAM framework. Figure below illustrates SAM tool decision framework for SAM.

Tool Decision framework for SAM

In order achieve your organization's Level IV SAM maturity goals, it is imperative to analyze tools that can automate your day-to-day tasks to improve accuracy with less or no manual intervention. One of the core aspects of tool is the ability to consolidate licenses inventory, replenishments and manage subsequent forecasts with current licenses position. This would help you in normalization of licenses based on the procured vs. actual consumption analysis real-time. Hence, you will be able to present dashboard with complete traceability details of an asset position and share it with the steering committee to quicken decision making. This would enable your alignment with the landscape roadmap and plans to procure more licenses based on the actual usage. Hence, you can be on the driver seat during the negotiation with the respective editor.

SAM Best practices

SAM tool encompasses the entire lifecycle of SAM processes:

g. Inventory
h. Reconcile
i. Share
j. Discover
k. Normalize
l. Optimize

Disruptive Technology Trends

There are three key trends prominent across organizations today which are increasing the need for software asset management:

1. **Digital Transformation:** This refers to the shift in workflows, services, and operations across organizations to meet demands of consumers and employees. This ultimately allows for greater accessibility and efficiency by digital means. As organizations increase digital assets to meet these needs, they need increasing of SAM to monitor these assets throughout their lifecycle.

2. **Cloud:** As software "as a Service" (SaaS) models become the new norm, software assets are moved out of the traditional datacenter and into the cloud. This can diminish visibility into deployed assets, while the consumption of software without installation makes it more difficult to monitor software compliance. The risk of overspend is very prevalent when utilizing cloud technologies without the correct monitoring tools.

3. **Cybersecurity:** has become a major concern for all businesses. SAM helps monitor software assets and their maintenance to ensure they are updated and not vulnerable to cyberattacks.

As organizations optimize their operations to adapt to these key trends, SAM tools will be necessary in monitoring increasing numbers of applications and solutions in a manageable and efficient way.

The IT industry is undergoing a significant digital revolution. Granted, this revolution makes life easier for end users, but as IT Managers, our lives are only getting more complex as we strive to adapt to this ever-changing landscape.

Below are 5 trends affecting the SAM industry:

1. AUDIT: Increasing Audit Trend by Editors

The most notable SAM trend would be the increased rate of publisher audits. We've written many times on various tactics you can use to prepare yourself for the inevitable audit but understand that publishers use the audit to retain their revenue streams. This audit may be an additional revenue streams for editors or a real intent to avoid non-compliance. In either case, customers should be nimble in responding to the audit requirements with ability to forecast.

With the increased focus on audits to drive revenue, publishers are not focusing on selling new product to new customers, thus decreasing their pool of customers to audit. Publishers also tend to audit customers more than once, as suggested by a 2007 Gartner survey.

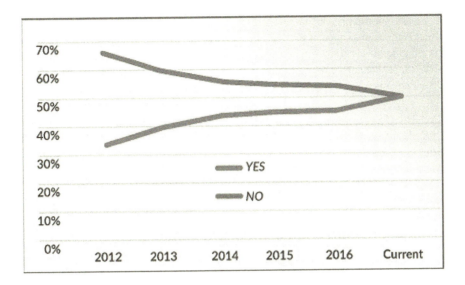

Source: ISACA Survey

The above ISACA IT audit benchmarking survey reports an increased trend of I.T audit by the respective editors. IT Audit role is expanding with exponential increase in major technology initiatives and IT audit's growth role in supporting them. Most organizations include cyber security as part of the audit plan.

2. TECHNOLOGY: Increased complexity in licensing

Customers discovered that running discrete, stand-alone servers and data centres across the world is less economically feasible than going to servers that can be carved up into smaller virtual servers. In other words, Virtualization is driving the need for unique SAM skills.

With increasing Virtual Machines, it's much harder to track the license accurately and track those changes going on as that server farm grows. Therefore, virtualization is driving complexity in licensing metrics because virtualization is what you need to deliver cloud. Forward-thinking cloud software providers "rent" software to organizations via a Monthly License Charge (MLC).

In 2018 nearly 40% of enterprise IT decision makers identified public cloud as their top priority. Business leaders want IT services that will ensure their organizations are ahead of the digital transformation curve. As an alternative to developing these services in house, IT departments are looking for cloud platforms that can provide more cost-efficient, flexible services without sacrificing enterprise requirements for performance, reliability, security, and regulatory compliance.

Take the below graphic, for example:

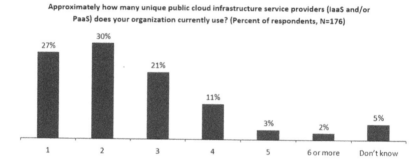

Source: Enterprise Strategy Group, 2017.

While the large Cloud Service Providers are competing for domination in the enterprise cloud service market, a recent ESG survey shows that instead of adapting a single CSP, many organizations are moving to a multi-cloud infrastructure, taking advantage of unique CSP capabilities while preventing being locked into a specific CSP environment. As you can see in the following figure, over 50% of companies surveyed are using more than one CSP and 15% are using 4 or more CSPs.

3. GLOBALIZATION: Revised sourcing

Most companies are finding that because they're globalized, and they have tax benefits for buying software in specific countries, then moving that software to where they really need it creates a level of procurement complexity that also adds to the SAM challenge. They buy it in one country, use the software in another and are often surprised when the publisher demands they have maintenance/support in the country they bought it from.

Simply put, organizations see they can purchase the same piece of software for a far less price and greater tax cut in one country, but they're not thinking about the maintenance/support implications for those applications.

4. SOFTWARE: CLOUD & BYOD

We all know about Cloud and bring your own device (BYOD) adaption challenges. It's more of an industry trend as opposed to software itself. Cloud/BYOD is moving towards a consumption model, which does away with the old days where customers typically bought large quantities of software and had to plan huge capital expenditure to account for the volume licenses and expected discounts for their purchases. Now, they're purchasing per device, per user, or per month. This presents several challenges to a traditional IT manager:

- They're no longer paying for software, they're paying for a service.
- The same applications that reside on your desktop can also be found in your pocket.
- The line between "corporate owned assets" and "personal assets" is becoming blurred.
- Do I track the software, or does my service provider track it?

Certain cloud providers will supply a suite of software while you bring complementary software of your own, which creates a mix of software assets. The infrastructure suite, OS, database engine, and web server engine are all provided by the cloud provider, but certain tools and application design suites, etc., may require a third party.

Best Practices

Like with all projects or new initiatives, there needs to be a business justification and a general case for implementing new processes, procedures and disciplines. There are several routes that an organization can follow to build up a business justification for SAM, dependent on what the end goal is.

The idea of building a business justification for SAM can be a process that can happen at any point during a SAM project. You may be asked to present the benefits of SAM at the initial 'buy-in' stage, or it may be a process that senior management wishes to go through on a yearly basis, so they can see the organization are still reaping the benefits of having a SAM structure in place.

Dependent on the maturity stage of your SAM project, the business justification can either be a huge document highlighting where SAM will impact (and benefit) the organization, or it could simply be an update on what benefits SAM has had over the past year. Either way, it is important for the SAM team to keep in regular contact with senior management, so they know and understand how the SAM team impact the organization in a positive manner.

Before Selecting Your SAM Tool

Before focusing on SAM tools and features, it is first important to address the infrastructure that must already be in place for a successful SAM program. SAM, by definition, is the necessary people, processes, and technology for effective management of software assets. Therefore, before moving into the tool selection stage, there must be a SAM team in place to manage the tool, and processes in place which will allow the information collected and presented by the tool effective.

Next, the SAM team will have to thoroughly assess what they specifically need out of their SAM tool. Every organization will have different needs based on their size, the publishers they use, and their IT environment.

The SAM team will have to consider what kind of tool and features will best align with their processes and organizational needs. For example, should your organization use an agent or non-agent-based SAM discovery tool? This refers to the method of inventory collection, and whether an agent installed on each computer collects and monitors inventory, versus a non-agent network-based approach to asset discovery.

Selecting a SAM Tool to Meet Digital Initiatives

Once the SAM team is aligned on the functionality for the tool to be effective and successful, they can begin the process of researching and selecting their SAM tool. This process will vary and be subjective based on the needs of the organization. However, there are a few features that organizations should keep in mind as they aim to align their SAM program with modern business initiatives, including: intelligence, automation and visibility.

Financial impact

One of the main reasons for organizations to invest in SAM is the understanding that having a successful program can have on an organization bottom line. There are several key financial impacts that SAM have on an organization. The amount of money that can be saved on software and hardware by implementing SAM processes can be huge and make a real difference to how an organization views software and hardware.

When initially implementing a SAM project within an organization the impact on the bottom line will be dramatic and may give a false indication as to how much money can be saved year-on-year with SAM. The first few years are going to be extremely fruitful to those organizations just starting off with SAM as they will make savings on their monthly software spend, there may be savings made on hardware and savings made through the renegotiation process with software agreements (including support and maintenance on software). Whilst this is all a good advert for SAM, it isn't realistic to think that any organization will save millions each year.

Once the initial savings are made, and compliancy is starting to be addressed then the focus shifts to maintaining compliancy, standardizing software and reducing or stabilizing the software and hardware budgets. The SAM team may not be able to present huge savings to the board each quarter, but they will be able to show their worth in other areas, such as streamlined processes, quicker service desk response for software related issues and a reduction in new software requests. They can also present any 'license pools' they may have generated through internal audits or reviews. Once a SAM team has achieved something approaching a "steady state", it can then start to focus on ensuring that more strategic business ambitions are realized.

Audit challenges

A key phrase within software asset management is 'being audit ready'. Audits are the buzzword now and all organizations should be aware of the implications from a bad audit. Being audit ready and ensuring you are managing your compliancy levels are a huge factor towards the success of a SAM project. Having a bad audit experience cannot only result in huge cost implications, but also in a damaged reputation, which may have long-term ramifications for the adoption of SAM in your company.

There have been several high-visibility audits in recent times, with court cases making claims for nine-figure damages. Auditing is a serious business, and rightly so. Organizations wouldn't dare steal a laptop or tablet for use within their organization, so why should they use software that they don't have a license for?

Software asset management will help soften the blow to an organization, should they be audited, both from a financial standpoint but also from a resource point of view. It will also help organizations be prepared for the audit processes and have some idea of any discrepancies they may have. If there are any instances of non-compliance, then SAM processes will help the organization make the required changes to become compliant.

SAM is becoming a core business function

SAM is quickly becoming a core business function that is a must for all organizations to have. It has gone from being 'nice to have' and 'something an organization should do' to a discipline that impacts all areas of the organization and has a big say in major organizational decisions. Software asset management not only assists the successes of other IT functions, such as service management, but it also helps with other functions such as procurement, finance and overall strategic planning.

Due to the importance of SAM it should be considered when making any key business decisions. There needs to be a SAM representative on the board so that they are kept up to date and have a say in any major decisions or strategies that the organization makes. This way the SAM team can prepare for any changes and update anything related to SAM processes or licensing.

Core SAM Processes

Process / Policy	What does it do?
Software use	Highlights what users are permitted to do with any software installed on their machine. Any mis-use could result in disciplinary action.
Software procurement	The correct process for purchasing new software instances.
Software authorization and deployment	The process for new software requests and the correct approval/deployment process.
Starters, movers and leavers	What should happen with software when a new starter starts, if someone moves department or office and what happens to the software asset when someone leaves.
Disaster recovery	In the result of a disaster, mission critical IT services are maintained until the disaster is deemed over.
Software recycling	Ensures the right methods are followed when re-distributing or recycling a software license following someone leaving or an internal software license review.
License Compliance	Ensures license compliancy is met, and that any non-compliance issues are addressed quickly and efficiently.

There are several other processes that you can implement to ensure the success of a SAM project, but the six processes above are the core group that a SAM project needs to be built around. It is important to get processes created, approved and implemented as soon as the agreement for a SAM project has been given. The success of any SAM estate is primarily down to the successful implementation of said processes and having the correct personnel in place to ensure that the processes are followed and abided by.

The core SAM processes need to be implemented at the first stage of a SAM project, with communication and direction coming from senior management. It's never easy implementing new processes within an organization, and it may take users time to understand and start following these modified/new ways of working. However, if education and constant communication is provided then eventually the core SAM processes will become business as usual. The core SAM processes need to be updated regularly to consider changes with technology or internal changes with IT and procurement. Ensure that the processes are evaluated and updated every six to nine months.

It's also important to note that implementing the core SAM processes can help save a large amount of money when it comes to software agreements. Having processes in place will allow you to have full control over the contract negotiations and can understand current and future requirements to ensure there isn't any over spend on software. This is looked at further in the 'building a business justification' section.

For a more in-depth look and explanation of the core SAM

Asset Management practices

Senior Management support

One of, if not the most important factor when implementing software asset management, is gaining senior management support. Without having the buy-in from senior management and support from a high level the project won't take off or become a success. The backing and support of senior management is also a sign to other staff members and departments that software asset management is to be taken seriously and that the organization is committed and dedicated to the support of a SAM project.

Senior management can also help with the overall implementation of SAM. They can work with the SAM team to provide support and direction from the top, so that the SAM project can work towards and align with the overall strategy and goals of the organization. Whilst the day-to-day running of the SAM project will be down to the SAM professionals, the overall responsibility of the project and of the software assets and compliancy rests with senior management, so it is in their interests to have an interest in the SAM project and strive to ensure it is a success.

Communication and Education

Another key factor to consider when implementing software asset management is to communicate and educate all users within the organization about SAM and what the overall goal of the project is. This also helps our next step in creating the right environment for a SAM project to thrive in. What needs to be remembered is that SAM is a programmer, not a project - something that needs to be considered a living thing, so it needs to be managed daily.

Providing communication to end users about the SAM project will go a long way to achieving general buy-in. End users don't need to know everything about the SAM project, but communicating regular briefs on the SAM projects progress will help users see the benefits of SAM and the progress being made. The SAM team could also communicate licensing changes with IT staff and heads of department. This could be information regarding changes to the license metrics, compliancy changes, terms of use changes or even information regarding Enterprise or Global agreements that the organization has entered.

Furthermore, it's also good to host several SAM and licensing WebEx sessions or workshops. These workshops and virtual sessions can educate users on the basics of SAM and software licensing, or even advanced deep dive sessions that going into more specifics or more complex aspects of software licensing. What has worked well in the past for global organizations is to host two of the same sessions at different times, one in the morning and one in the evening for users in different time zones. Consider the workshops as the chance for the SAM team to sell SAM and its benefits to the users, but also as an outlet for highlighting the benefits of SAM and what implementing SAM will achieve.

Creating the right environment

It is also important to create a SAM ethos within the organization's environment. Users need to have the correct SAM mentality when it comes to software, software requests and software usage. Creating the right environment can naturally happen with the right education and communication methods. This helps with the day-to-day interaction between the SAM team and the end users. Having the right environment and mentality can mean a dramatic difference in response in certain situations:

Finding the right solution

There are several SAM tools currently on the market to assist with a SAM project. Finding the right solution for the organization is a project and takes time and careful consideration. Firstly, the organization must ask themselves several questions:

Compatibility with other systems/solutions/tools within your environment.

Will you get support from the tool vendor? You'll certainly need it!

1. What impact will implementation have on users?
2. How easy it is to deploy an inventory agent within your environment? (presuming the SAM tool needs an inventory agent to gather inventory data)
3. Do you have the resources to manage the tool daily?
4. Do you have the server infrastructure to host such a powerful tool?
5. Licensing models are changing. Does the tool manage cloud software (both public and private cloud) or web-based software?
6. How often does the tool vendor release patches or new features? Will not updating impact on your existing solutions performance?
7. How is the data gathered? Is there 'down time' whilst the data is being updated? Will this impact on certain users? (Time-zone based issue).
8. It is important to consider a variety of SAM solution providers. Ask them to come into your place of work and demo their product and check online for reviews and customer feedback. Most importantly don't be blinded by the promises of the salesman!

Highlighting the cost savings

One of the biggest justifications for software asset management is the savings that can be made on software spend.

Initial cost savings

The initial cost savings of SAM have the potential to be huge. Obviously, this is dependent on what the organization's software estate looks like before implementing SAM. Either way, there will be large savings on both hardware and software during the initial months and years of a SAM project. The major savings, and an attractive justification for senior management are:

Savings made by utilizing existing software licenses (removing unused applications, removing the wrong versions installed, recycling licenses, creating 'license pools')

- Savings made on software agreements
- Savings made on maintenance and support agreements
- Reduced software spending
- Reduced hardware spending (successful SAM can impact on hardware savings)

To successful make those initial savings, the SAM team need the support from senior management to enforce the processes and procedures required to actively make said savings. Senior management need to be the ones orchestrating the changes and dictating to other employees at the organization that they must comply with helping the SAM team by allowing them to remove any unused or in appropriate software.

Away from savings made, the initial SAM project can also get rid of software the organization has deemed to be on the 'blacklist' such as games, gambling software, trial licenses or legacy software that is no longer supported. It also allows the organization to standardize the software that they want to use and support moving forward.

Realistic cost savings

After the first few years of implementing a SAM structure and having all the software and licensing processes in place, the cost savings will not be as great as they were at the start of the project. The main financial aim and justification of SAM is the reduction in software and hardware spend or budgets, and several examples

147

in which the SAM team have saved money through recycling a license or providing a cheaper alternative.

It is at this stage in which senior management that are driven by money and cost savings start to question the need for SAM. The SAM team need to highlight the reduction in software budgets since the introduction of SAM, the improved compliancy figures since the introduction of SAM and the ease in which software is now requested, procured, managed and then retired thanks to SAM processes. If senior management can see that SAM processes save a lot of time and money, even with the practice being established within the organization, then there is no reason for support to waiver.

Effective license management

In our case study, client had started with Level (I) maturity and gradually progressed their way to Level (III) by implementing license best practices using tools, accelerators and methods. It is important to manage licenses and software assets for compliance, audit and optimization to save costs. To do that, organizations will need robust practices, governance to manage licenses by avoiding risks that may escalate from time-to-time.

To maintain current license position, SAM Manager would launch audit internally to identify the non-compliance and take appropriate measures to mitigate risks due to non-compliance. However, not limited to the risk mitigation plan, SAM team will be responsible to drive technical teams to upgrade software asset to save costs with an up-to-date inventory of active users in the system. Together with cost savings is the fact that software licenses are more likely to be utilized and optimized with a SAM structure in place. 'License Pools' can be created to ensure that money isn't spent unnecessarily on software licenses, and that a 'pool' of licenses can be used should a request come in for that piece of software. 'License Pools' reduce the amount of waiting time a user has to endure when requesting a new piece of software and can also improve the speed in which some projects start or finish.

Furthermore, effective license management can help the organization to streamline and standardize the software that they make available to end-users. As mentioned previously this is also a cost saving method. Knowing exactly what software is required and having all the licenses being used and utilized, the organization is in a great negotiating position with vendors for renewals or new license agreements.

Effective license management also helps without next point, being audit ready. Knowing exactly what licenses is needed, and what may be required in the future helps organizations establish their ELP (effective license position). Knowing your ELP and presenting a compliancy report to senior management is another strong reason to implement SAM. Highlighting any discrepancies with licenses before the implementation of SAM, and then regular compliancy reports once SAM has been implemented will further enhance the justification for SAM.

Audit prep & readiness using Digital

Finally, a key justification that will make senior management sit up and take notice is the fact that implementing a successful SAM project will help the organization be 'audit ready'. This is a key topic to discuss as most of the organizations are reactive to the audit requirements imposed by the editors. Hence, you lose their credibility and a strong negotiation position if you're not geared up in advance for the audit requirements by editor. There are even more repercussions, if you are identified by the respective editor as non-compliant as you would lose the opportunity to strongly negotiate and your reputation would go for a toss. Just imagine a large public company identified as non-compliant, which would damage your corporate reputation with the public and your stock value may go down.

It is common for auditors end up charging huge fines and coming away with a 'financial win', then they are likely to communicate this with their counterparts at another vendor. This results in a vicious cycle of audits for the company and a lot of public humiliation. It will also result in many fines and licenses that will need to be purchased to rectify any non-compliance. There is a lot of upheaval during an audit with employees unable to do their jobs.

Without SAM the organization will have a reactive attitude, which basically means 'drop everything and respond to the audit. In the digital landscape, you should have real-time data to present to the auditors with absolutely no additional efforts required during the external audit process. It should be as simple as publishing the dashboard with real-time inventory and consumption details to them without much efforts. This should create a good view of your organization readiness in front of the editors and help you effectively negotiate subsequent deals with them.

SAM and software licensing

SAM and software licensing are two different disciplines, but they intertwine with each other in so many ways that software licensing is often considered identical to SAM. In our case study, these two functions were managed by SAM Manager.

Software licensing

A software license is a legal agreement between the software vendor (copyright holder) and the end user that defines the rights to what they can and cannot do with the application. There are several different licensing metrics. They include (but are not exclusive to):

License Metric	Description
Academic	License specifically for Academic institutes. License must be used in accordance with the terms and conditions specified for academic use.
Annual License	Yearly license agreement. Contractual agreement between vendor and customer.
Capacity Based License	License is based on the capacity of the CPU/Hard Drive or other hardware configuration elements.
Click Through License	Usually related to software that is downloaded from the internet. Also related to the click-through agreement when installing software. Before installation the user must click through the license agreement to agree to comply.
Client Access License (CAL)	Allows users to connect to server software to use the software's features/functions
Cloud Credits	Cloud credits are the unit of measurement required to perform certain tasks or rights to run certain applications provided by the vendor. Hosted in the cloud.
License Metric	Description
Concurrent License	Multiple users can access the software at the same time. Can also be referred to as

	a 'Network License'
Enterprise License	Enterprise (all company owned sites/departments) is defined in a license agreement.
Font License	Font specific license. Specific to types.
Freeware	License requires no purchase, but the copyrights are still held by the developer. Developer can sell the software in the future and does not distribute the source code.
Public License (GPL)	License and software available for free. Allows users to use, share, copy and modify the software.
Machine based license	Also known as a 'device license'. License is locked to the machine.
Named user license	License is assigned to a named user who must be identified to ensure the license agreement is validated.
Network License	License that covers machines that are on the same network infrastructure.
Open Source license	Free for use, but with restrictions. EULA and terms of use should be checked before use.
Processor Based	Also known as 'CPU based'. Relates to licensing the overall capacity of the device or the processors in the device.
Site License	Single license that covers a whole site. Sites can be defined from a whole country to a single floor or department.
Subscription License	License only available during time of subscription. No rights to use it pre or post agreement dates (unless agreement renewed).

Trial License	Can also be known as 'Shareware License'. The software may be tried for a set period before purchase or removal.
Upgrade License	Upgrade from older version to a newer version of an application. Incentives are provided by the vendor to try and push the upgrade.
Volume license	Several licenses are purchased during a single transaction.

There are other license types, but they are not as common as those listed above. Licensing can be extremely complicated and if not completely understood it can leave the company in a financial mess. If licenses are not managed correctly, and if there are any instances of non-compliancy (where there is an install or user without a license) then the potential fallout from an audit could be hugely damaging, both financially and towards the company's reputation.

Two sides of the Coin!

In our case study, we observed SAM manage all software assets with respective teams responsible for supporting software license current position. Often, SAM manager consolidated dashboard with inputs from different license experts, who're the technical teams managing the software asset. A typical organization does not have the luxury of having both a SAM and Software Licensing department, so they assign the responsibility of license management to the SAM team. This makes sense, as the SAM team are responsible for the overall management of the software asset, so they should also be responsible for the license and ensuring that the terms and conditions of the license are not broken.

Having the license management aspect incorporated into the SAM team obviously means that more work and pressure is added to the SAM personnel, but that option is far better for the organization than having individual departments or users managing their own licenses. Another way in which SAM and software licensing can work together is if an organization assigns a certain 'super user' of the software to be the software's spokesperson for the organization. The overall responsibility for the license and its compliancy remains with the SAM team, but the software spokesperson will be the first point of contact for any queries relating to the software.

SAM Organization was discussed in the earlier chapters, I our case study, we managed SAM Organization as mentioned below:

The Program Director is responsible for policy reinforcements with SAM managers responsible for respective functions with the group by interacting with compliance (legal) and other functions to consolidate data. The flexible teams were responsible for support each of the SAM managers in terms of current license position to comply with requirements. SAM managers were responsible for the licenses position along with the flexible resources, who supported the usage details with entitlements. Overall dashboard was managed by the respective SAM managers and consolidated into one view for the SAM Director review and inputs monthly.

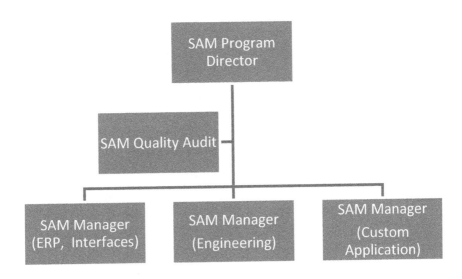

This in turn reduces some of the pressure and workload on the SAM team. They can then focus on their daily SAM tasks, and the overall management of software licenses, rather than being a software 'helpdesk' and expected to know what all the software installed on their estate does and what features it has.

Critical Success Factors

With the increased complexities in the landscape, it is important to establish SAM framework with the experts to manage software assets and license compliances. Often leadership teams overlook SAM initiatives to find non-compliance during the audit with respective editors. This may lead to a penalty or legal challenges with the editor as often auditors search of evidences of non-compliance. In most of the cases, editors may take this opportunity to sell additional licenses or perhaps help you regain compliance with additional licenses procurement. However, if you're identified as non-compliance, you may not be able to effectively negotiate with the respective editor. Software asset and license

153

compliance are critical success factors to support your organization with compliance status and maintain a good negotiation position with the editors.

Tools & Accelerators

On the bright side, <u>SAM tool vendors are becoming more refined</u>, with rich and integrated functionality on their SAM tools. Gone are the days when you had to build your spreadsheet to track your entitlement and run publisher specific applications to gather inventory data and then do the mashup/correlation of that data manually. Now there are whole suites of tools that will store that data and do those comparisons for you. You can combine SAM dashboard tools with the editor specific tools to build the final dashboard real-time. For example, in our case study, client managed to build a dashboard using QlikView to publish quarterly audit & compliance report with risk KPI's measured. However, in the background for NAMED Direct analysis, team used SAP USMM standard procedures and the editor specific tools to measure usage such as Microsoft, Dassault specific tools to extract most reliable usage data with entitlements, which was further integrated with QlikView to publish comprehensive real-time dashboard for auditor's review.

And they're smart enough to know the bigger publishers licensing metrics. They can determine whether a discovery is a processor or user-based license and compare it using the right metrics. I recommend for organizations to move to these integrated tool suites to help them refine their analysis.

Regardless of what intelligence your SAM tool collects, the result will be a huge amount of data and intelligence. Automation will be a key feature for modern SAM tools to assist in making all this intelligence actionable in a reasonable period. As critical business functions become more reliant on software and applications, there will be little patience for drawn out license approval processes, which might result in employees circumventing SAM teams altogether.

SAM must be a continual process, not something that is only considered in the face of an audit. Tools that can automate software maintenance, software requests and access, device enrollment, and more will help ensure that SAM moves at the pace of modern organizations and help to ensure SAM processes are not ignored. For example. Flexera can help you build a great dashboard with editor usage analysis.

Licensing in Hybrid Environments

While many organizations still use on-premises software assets, they are also increasing their use of cloud-based SaaS applications. It is a common misconception that SAM is not necessary in the cloud, as these licenses are easily scaled based on consumption. However, this is not the case. To monitor spend, governance, and asset maintenance, organizations need a SAM tool that has visibility into, and can collect data on, assets in the cloud. To make this information more manageable, organizations will want to look for a SAM tool that correlates the data from on-premises assets and cloud assets into a single view to understand the overall software estate.

Today, SAM is more necessary than ever as modern organizations increase their software assets to keep up with competitive trends and employee and consumer needs. For SAM to be effective in these transitioning environments, organizations will need a team and process in place, as well as a SAM tool that incorporates these features uniquely suited to modern enterprise initiatives.

SAM is becoming more important to organizations and is a vital aspect towards organizations successes. Any member of the organization that uses a computer, device or piece of software is a customer of SAM. They are using a product or device that falls under the management of the SAM discipline, so organizations have a duty to have clear, defined and dynamic SAM processes.

Being pro-active with your SAM program is the best way to be. Obviously, there may be challenges or situations that arise that require you to be reactive, but even then, the SAM team will be better prepared for such events. The idea of being pro-active is that you are completely on top of your SAM estate, and you are prepared for any eventuality. This includes the creation of mature SAM processes, having the right tool in place for your organization, and having clear roles and responsibilities for SAM and SAM staff.

Summary

As mentioned throughout this chapter, an organization cannot function without a robust software asset management practice with tools, accelerators. This would ensure asset lifecycle is managed with every employee as a customer of SAM, if they use a piece of software or an application. That software asset needs to be managed correctly throughout its lifecycle, and that's where SAM comes in. You may want to achieve a desired level (3) or (4) align with your core objectives. It is essential to manage assets effectively to save costs in the long run, as we discussed evolution of your I.T landscape in the digital era.

Now, it is the right time to fasten your seat belts with the best-in-class software asset management practices to achieve Level (4) SAM maturity to stay ahead of the competition to keep all stakeholders happy.

■   ■   ■

www.ingramcontent.com/pod-product-compliance
Lightning Source LLC
Chambersburg PA
CBHW031240050326

40690CB00007B/892